P9-CAB-131

# Cooking Club

## Great Ideas & Delicious Recipes for Fabulous Get-Togethers

Dina Guillen *and* Michelle Lowrey

SASQUATCH BOOKS
SEATTLE

FAIRMONT BRANCH LIBRARY
4330 Fairmont Pkwy.
Pasadena TY 77504-3306

FOR THE KITCHEN TABLE COOKING CLUB—MARIA, CAROLYN, LISA, CINDY, AND NICOLE

Copyright © 2009 by Dina Guillen and Michelle Lowrey
All rights reserved. No portion of this book may be reproduced or utilized in any form, or by any electronic, mechanical, or other means, without the prior written permission of the publisher.

Printed in China
Published by Sasquatch Books
Distributed by PGW/Perseus
15 14 13 12 11 10 09          10 9 8 7 6 5 4 3 2 1

Cover design: Rosebud Eustace
Front photograph of authors Michelle Lowrey (l) and Dina Guillen (r) with members of the Kitchen Table Cooking Club by Emily Nathan
Interior design and composition: Rosebud Eustace
Interior photographs: Kate Baldwin

Library of Congress Cataloging-in-Publication Data
Guillen, Dina.
  Cooking club : great ideas & delicious recipes for fabulous get-togethers / Dina Guillen and Michelle Lowrey.
    p. cm.
  Includes index.
  ISBN-13: 978-1-57061-560-3
  ISBN-10: 1-57061-560-8
  1. Entertaining. 2. Cookery. 3. Menus. I. Lowrey, Michelle. II. Title.
  TX731.G79 2009
  641.5
                      2008048829

**Sasquatch Books**
119 South Main Street, Suite 400
Seattle, WA 98104
(206) 467-4300
www.sasquatchbooks.com
custserv@sasquatchbooks.com

# Contents

# Acknowledgments

First and foremost, we would like to thank the members of our cooking club: Maria Everly, Carolyn Soriano, Lisa Frazzetta, Cindy LaCasse, and Nicole Baker. Words alone will never be enough to thank you for the incredible experience of being part of this cooking club and what it has brought to each of us. You have shared your lives, and opened your hearts. We have laughed—as well as cried—together for all these years. We consider ourselves beyond fortunate to call each of you such dear friends and we dedicate this book to you.

We want to thank our dear friends Bonnie Bussard and Dolly Sood for sharing your beloved and treasured family recipes with us. And a huge thank you to Dave and Kate Kaufman, and Jeff and Kim Ball for giving us honest and critical feedback on recipes when we requested it.

A special thank you to Biba Caggiano for her advice and guidance.

To our parents Sherry and Dennis, Ghazi and Sylvia, who taught us that cooking and entertaining is the ultimate expression of love.

And most of all, to our husbands and children, Corey, Roland, Andrew, Collin, and Riley. You always believe in us, support us, and encourage us in everything we do. And for that, we are most grateful. We love you.

# Introduction

Ever since the thirteenth century, groups of people have come together to form cooking clubs (also called supper clubs) for the purpose of trying new recipes, improving their cooking skills, and ultimately establishing lifelong friendships. Today, all across the country, all kinds of cooking clubs are being formed, including diet-support clubs, gourmet clubs, charity-based clubs, recipe-swapping clubs, adventurous eating clubs, neighborhood cooking clubs, all-male cooking clubs, all-female cooking clubs, couples cooking together clubs, singles-only clubs, and everything in between. In our fast-paced, eating-on-the-run culture, more and more people are interested in slowing down, gathering with friends, and cooking and eating together in a more intimate and social setting.

## Is a Cooking Club Right for Me?

Are you so preoccupied with food that you have a budget just for cheese? Do you carry your own homemade spice blend around with you in your car? Are the only dreams that you remember those that involve food? Do you keep a handmade cozy over your barbecue tools when they are not in use? Did you get upset at your spouse on your birthday because he bought you earrings instead of the baking set that you asked for? If you answered yes to more than one of these questions, you are a bona fide food geek.

Don't take offense at the term! We place all people who live and breathe food in this category and consider them some of the coolest folks around. We're food geeks, too, and we wear the title with pride. Still not convinced that you are a food geek? We bet that the only organized room in your house is the kitchen and that you are not sure that the other rooms in your house are actually necessary.

Food geeks can't stay closeted for long, though. They need to mingle and share their love of food with others. That is why starting a cooking club is such a great idea, and this book will help you get going. Being a part of such a group is a wonderful experience and a great way to satisfy that urge to get creative in the kitchen. By bringing together your friends or other people who share a common interest, you get the best of both worlds. You get to eat a great meal while becoming a better chef in your own kitchen, and you get to socialize and bond with others like you: fellow food geeks—the people who eat to live and live to eat, and who always seem to find each other. In these pages we will give you the tools, tips, and information to get you started on your own cooking club adventure.

You don't have to be completely fanatical about cooking, either. We live in an age and a place where cooking from scratch is no longer very common. Cooking clubs are becoming more popular with people who want to get back to the basics and eat a beautifully prepared home-cooked meal among friends. Simply wanting to get some friends together to try out some new recipes you found in a magazine is great, too.

Call it what you will—a cooking club, a supper club, or a gourmet group— these gatherings have been all the rage for years, especially since the rise of the Food Network, cooking magazines like *Cooking Light, Gourmet, Bon Appétit, Saveur,* and others, and culinary Web sites like Epicurious.com, Chowhound.com, and eGullet.org, to name a few.

Now, we love eating at fine-dining restaurants as much as the next person, but this book is for those of you who want to do the actual cooking and entertaining. There is something special about entertaining in your own home, with the smell of mouth-watering foods wafting from the oven, fresh flowers and candles on the table, your favorite music playing on your stereo, and good friends to share it with. Cooking as a group in the kitchen, collaborating on a dish while debating who is the best chef on television, strengthens friendships and builds your cooking and entertaining expertise in a way that no restaurant outing can.

## Who We Are and How We Got Started

Allow us first to introduce ourselves, and to let you know how our group came into being. We are two members of a Sacramento-area cooking club called The Kitchen Table Cooking Club. Our cooking club has been going strong since 2001, when Maria Everly founded it. Maria had been part of a cooking club that focused on healthy, light, and quick meals, and over time, she found herself more and more interested in the intricacies and science of food and cooking. She asked Michelle Lowrey to help her form a cooking club that focused on gourmet cooking, and gradually they began asking friends to join.

Along the way, we all were invited by someone in the club who wanted to expand this group of women. We were fast becoming friends while developing our cooking skills. Some of us were new stay-at-home moms who had recently quit our jobs to be home with the kids, and we desperately wanted an outlet—any outlet. Others wanted something to do besides going home from the office and watching the latest episode of *The Real Housewives of Orange County*. Living in suburbia has its advantages, but we all craved an authentic social network of friends—away from the kids, away from the office, and away from the "real housewives" we saw on television.

Our cooking club represents many different facets of what it means to be a woman living in the United States today. The group is composed of driven career women, working mothers, and stay-at-home moms. Some of us have children and some don't, but we are all living out our own versions of the American dream—whether that is 2.3 kids, a mortgage, and a hamster, or marriage with no kids and catering to a very spoiled dog. One thing's for sure, though: we've got class, we can be a little crass, and we serve it all up with an extra side of sass!

Our group of super-hip chicks consists of Carolyn Soriano, Lisa Frazzetta, Nicole Baker, Cindy LaCasse, Dina Guillen, Michelle Lowrey, and the aforementioned Maria Everly. We all have work responsibilities inside and outside the home and are doing the best we can to bring up our children (and husbands). And while some of us are more domestic than others, we all love to cook and entertain, and we can make a mean lemon-drop martini. Just don't expect us to go all domestic and serve it up wearing a lacy apron, pearls, and high heels à la June Cleaver. Seriously, who's got the time? We're too busy scraping gum off the couch or scooping a Barbie shoe out of the fish tank with one hand while finalizing a marketing plan with the other.

We all come from different backgrounds. Michelle used to work in the food industry, B.C. (before children); Nicole is a teacher; Lisa is the PTO treasurer of her kids' school; Carolyn owns a gymnastics center; and Cindy, aside from her full-time sales job, has a part-time catering business and used to work as a wine distributor. Maria is an automotive finance executive who was born in Mexico, and Dina is a marketing executive who was born in Saudi Arabia.

Despite our diverse backgrounds and careers, we have a few things in common, the most obvious being that we all love to cook. Love it. You will never leave any of our houses hungry. We all joined our cooking club with a passion for cooking, but with the exception of Michelle, who had had a successful career as a pastry chef, we had not really spent much time refining our culinary skills.

Learning to cook is not always a smooth and easy road. We've all had our share of embarrassing "fallen soufflé" stories, "smoke billowing out of the oven" stories, and "it was the recipe, not me" stories. But we just don't care. We love food; we love cooking; we love to laugh at the catastrophes; we love to drink before, during, and after we've laughed at the catastrophes; and we love getting together to share in the whole experience. Our Cooking club has sharpened our cooking expertise and fostered our love of learning the craft to the point where we can all say we are confident in our abilities. We can, and have, cooked an entire menu from *The French Laundry Cookbook*. We might not get hired by Thomas Keller any time soon (okay, ever), but we're just saying—we can do it.

Another thing we have in common is that we love to travel. We have all traveled extensively throughout our lives. Sometimes we plan our trips around culinary hot spots. Other times we pick our travel destinations, then research the local cuisine and restaurants before we leave. But it always comes down to the food. And when we get back, we can't wait for our next cooking club gathering to talk about our trip and report back to everyone about our culinary experiences and adventures, and, oh yeah, the sites. We mention this because we encourage you to allow your taste buds to venture beyond your comfort zone, and traveling forces you to do that. Even if it means simply traveling to your local Turkish restaurant, trying new cuisines is an important part of the learning process.

We are just like most people in this country; we have the same day-to-day problems everyone else has. We're not famous, we're not fabulously wealthy, and we don't show up for work in a limousine. Our kids fight, our husbands leave the toilet seats up from time to time, and our bosses still get on our nerves on occasion. But one thing is for sure: we all love to get together and bond over that perfectly baked loaf of bread and a nice merlot. Once a month we take time out of our hectic lives and indulge in some much-needed girl talk, which keeps us all sane—and it's much cheaper than therapy.

The food may be the bricks, but the people in this group have been the mortar. Gretchen Bernsdorff, co-author of our last cookbook, *The Plank Grilling Cookbook*, was a longtime cooking club member, but after she moved away in 2006, we have not been able to replace her. Every once in a while we invite guests to join us, but for the most part, we have formed such a tight bond that it is usually just the seven of us at each month's gathering. We have arrived at a certain comfort level and are unwilling to change things up. We agree on the things that really matter; we know how far we can go with our recipes and skill levels; our cooking abilities have progressed at a similar pace; and we are familiar with each other's food preferences and budgets. These are all important factors when you are in a club together, and they have helped lead us to our cohesive, comfortable, "it ain't broke so let's not mess with it" formula.

## Cooking Clubs—They're Not Just for Women

If you are of the guy persuasion, please do not give up and go away. Just because our group is of the estrogen variety doesn't mean this book is not for you. Cooking clubs are sprouting up all over the country with real and wannabe chefs of every kind. There are groups of couples, groups of just men, women-only groups like ours, and everything and anything in between. In fact, throughout this book, we profile different groups from around the country and share with you what other folks are doing at their gatherings.

All you need is an interest in cooking and willing friends and you are good to go.

We have learned so much from being in a cooking club. We have learned that to make the best french fries you need to fry them twice; that you should never boil stock or it will get cloudy; and to add enough sugar to your sorbet to make it creamy, not icy. We have learned how to entertain as our parents did when we were kids, how to make invitations Martha Stewart would be proud of, how to set a table for ten, and how to set up our kitchens for the easiest access to everything. It has been a wonderful ride, one that will be a part of us for the rest of our lives. Michel de Montaigne once said, "The art of dining well is no slight art, the pleasure not a slight pleasure." We could not agree more, and we learned that firsthand by being a part of a cooking club.

Best of all, we have learned how to be supportive and encouraging of each other. We have built friendships that will last the rest of our lives. Our husbands and children have built similar friendships as a result of our cooking club. The Kitchen Table Cooking Club is just one small group in a sea of food lovers everywhere, all of them doing tasty and creative things with food. When it comes to being in a cooking club, no one way is the "correct" way. Do what comes naturally to you and makes you and the rest of your group happy and motivated to keep coming. As long as there is laughter and good food, served with a smile and some willing participants, we approve.

We hope this book encourages you to start your own cooking club and guides you in building a group that will have as profound an impact on you as it has on us. So, how about it? Are you ready to take the plunge and start your own cooking club? You won't regret your decision, and you will be in for a fun ride. A culinary adventure awaits you!

## How to Use This Book

Consider this an idea book. In the next few pages you will find some steps you should take when setting up a club to ensure that it starts off on the right foot and lasts for some time. Once you've got your group going, check out the twelve suggested dinner themes we've included here, complete with menus, recipes, tips for entertaining, and more. Finally, we've included profiles of a variety of cooking clubs from around the country. Perhaps these will inspire you to develop your own group.

Please note that each menu has been tailored for a minimum of eight people, with eight courses including a mixed drink. Most of the courses, however, are for full servings. So feel free to convert these to tasting menus, serving only half the suggested amount, providing the club members with leftovers. We have a feeling there are people waiting for you back home, hoping you will return with some goodies from your dinner. If your cooking club has fewer than eight members, feel free to pick and choose the courses you would like to serve at your gathering. Also, almost all the recipes can easily be halved successfully. If you have more than eight members, you can team up on the dishes, especially the ones that require a separate sauce to complete the meal. Most importantly, have fun and do what works best for your group.

Finally, we hope our menus will also find a home outside your cooking club, perhaps in planning your next dinner party. One of the hardest jobs when throwing a dinner party can be choosing foods and courses that complement each other. We've taken care of that step for you, and we've included tips for decorating, creating the right atmosphere, and party favors, as well.

There are few things more satisfying than knowing you have brought good food and good times to the people you love and enjoy most. May this book help you to that end, and may you enjoy many delectable dinner parties in your future. And we wish you one heck of a delicious ride!

# Guidelines to Starting and Maintaining a Successful Cooking Club

## Start with a Plan

Being in a cooking club can be great fun, but it takes planning and setting ground rules from the beginning to ensure that your group will be successful. A group that is started with little thought or effort may last for a little while, but it will likely peter out before long if some basic concerns aren't addressed from the get-go.

No group comes without its set of challenges, and it wasn't always smooth sailing for us, either. We lost some members once they understood the time commitment required, others realized that their passion for food wasn't strong enough to keep them coming, and others simply moved away or lost interest. Those who have stayed with the group have stayed with a vengeance. Yes, we have been around a while, and our group is a cohesive unit, but it took planning and forethought to get it off the ground.

To get you started, we have written some tips and guidelines to help you make the most of your own cooking club adventure. And at the end of each of the book's themed menu chapters, we offer profiles of successful cooking clubs from around the country. You will be introduced to a different cooking club, read stories from members, and discover some of the many ways you might set up your own club. For example, one cooking club's primary purpose is to raise money for charity, while another invites a different professional chef each month to instruct them while they cook, and another comes up with dinner themes based on movies. Some clubs have co-hosting duties, while others have a sole host. Some have annual dues, some have monthly dues, and some, like ours, have no dues at all. There are many variables you may wish to consider to make your club meet your own particular interests.

## Gather Some Like-Minded Friends

Our first piece of advice: do your homework when getting a group of friends together to form your group. Try to picture how everyone will interact, and consider personality types and potential clashes. It is important that everyone involved can actually get along and be in the same room together.

The conservative pastor may not get along well with the biker who enjoys telling dirty jokes. The PETA member may not take too kindly to the avid hunter who likes to share stories of his latest kill while espousing the virtues of the NRA. Such scenarios can be a recipe for disaster, and a good time will be had by—none.

Gather a group of people with similar culinary interests and a common purpose. And, of course, they should love cooking and eating together. That friend of yours—the one who eats only beige foods—is simply not a contender. Choose people who have the potential to get along and play nice with each other.

Shared interests could be a starting point for determining who should be in your cooking club. A lot of our club's members have small children of the same age, and we share that as a common bond. That being said, variety is the spice of life: too many people with similar interests can become as stale as a hunk of moldy, old bread. Over time, you run out of things to talk about.

## Agree on Your Goals

This may sound obvious, but getting people to agree on what they want from the group, right from the beginning, will save a lot of headaches later.

If one member is fine with an appetizer of Cheez Whiz on crackers while another expects geoduck sashimi, someone is going to walk away sadly disappointed. You should also agree on how casual or formal you want the group to be. Are paper plates okay, or should fine cutlery be the order of the day?

Our club wanted to prepare foods that were not the usual things we would eat on a typical Tuesday night in front of the television. We wanted to explore the culinary realms of different cultures and to learn new cooking techniques. We all loved food and wanted to share spectacular meals with each other. But your group might prefer to focus on casual fare and easy, low-stress preparations, which is absolutely fine.

Or maybe you'd like a group that focuses mainly on wine, with the food taking a side role. Well, that's okay too, but make sure that everyone in your group is on the same page.

## WHAT KIND OF COOKING CLUB TO FORM?

Just as there are many kinds of people and personalities, there is an endless variety of cooking clubs just waiting to be created. Whether you are looking to form a cooking club based on fine dining or a club that is more casual and relaxed, the possibilities are limited only by your own imagination. What's the right kind of club for you? Here are some questions you should consider to help you organize your new club:

- **Social function:** Will your group be mostly about the camaraderie, socializing, or fundraising, or do you want a group that focuses on cooking?

- **Focus:** Do you want your group to have a particular focus? Healthy meals? Quick and easy dishes for family and friends that you can take home and enjoy for the coming month? Or do you want your group to focus on gourmet meals, or learning more about the craft of cooking?

- **Skill level:** What is your skill level, and how important is it to you that the other club members share that same skill level? Many clubs have members of a similar skill level so as to prevent beginners from being intimidated by the more expert cooks in the group. Other clubs prefer members of mixed skill levels so that more advanced cooks can mingle with the less skilled, ultimately encouraging learning.

## GROUP STRUCTURE

It is also important to decide on the basic structure of the group:

- **Size matters:** How many people should you have in the club? Do you want a large group, or would you rather keep it smaller and more intimate?

- **Size control:** Do you want to limit the number of members you'll have or leave it open?

## Give Your Club a Catchy Name

So, what should your group be called? You don't have to name your group, but it's a fun way to bring a certain identity to yourselves. Our group wasn't always The Kitchen Table Cooking Club. In the beginning, we were The Lemon Drops. When we first got together at a restaurant here in town to decide the particulars of our group, we were enjoying some great lemon-drop martinis. The drinks were poured fast and furious. By the end of the night we were pretty tipsy—okay, drunk (a perfect state of mind for brainstorming). All kinds of names shot back and forth that evening, and when someone said, "The Lemon Drops," it seemed perfect.

For a long time, at every monthly event, lemon-drop martinis were served as the welcome drink. As our group evolved, we wanted our name to represent more than the fun we had one drunken evening. Carolyn came up with The Kitchen Table Cooking Club, and we all responded with big smiles on our faces; it was perfect. We all believe that the kitchen is the heart of every home, and that more day-to-day living takes place at the kitchen table than anywhere else. The kitchen table evokes images of Sunday dinners with Grandma, or board games played with the family. If food is love, then the table is what that love is served on. We loved the name, and the coziness and heartfelt memories that it evokes have stuck with us ever since. So whether you call yourselves "The Hot Tamales" or "Men Who Cook," we hope that you'll have as much fun coming up with a name as we all did.

## Decide How Often the Club Will Meet

Our club prefers to meet once each month, usually on a Saturday or Sunday. With a volley of e-mails, or at a cooking club event itself, we coordinate the next date that we can all attend. There isn't a repeating set date for our meetings because we find that by being more flexible, most people are able to be there. We usually meet in the evening, but we like to mix it up and do breakfast or lunch once in a while, too. As long as all the members get prior notice of what the host has planned, it works out fine with us.

## MEETING TIMES AND DATES

Decide how often your club should meet. Once a month? Every other month? Do you want to meet primarily in the evenings or at lunchtime? On weekends or weekdays?

Often, cooking clubs choose a specific day each month, like the second Tuesday of the month. Other clubs prefer more flexibility and decide on the meeting date one or two months before the meeting based on everyone's schedules. Just make sure you choose a time and date that works for everyone in your group.

Next, it's time to come up with a rotating event schedule that lists who will be hosting each month. After each member has hosted one meeting, a new cycle begins.

## HOSTING RESPONSIBILITIES

Consider how the hosting duties will be handled. Is there a sole host or will you host in groups? Does the host prepare the menu? Does the host prepare the main entrée? Or is the host's sole responsibility to set up and clean up while other members bring dishes or groceries to the host's home?

We are proud to report that for as long as our club has been in existence, we have rarely had a month with no meeting (except December, which we take off every year for the holidays). If for some reason a person isn't able to host on her given month, she finds someone to switch with. We find that the system works pretty well.

## Assign a Secretary for the Group

Now that you have brought together a group of people who want to form a cooking club and have agreed on the goals of the group, it's time for the secretary to write up the bylaws. Okay, it's not pretty, nor is it fun, but a set of clear ground rules is very helpful for a new group. Decide collectively what you all want as a cooking club, and then put it into writing.

Be specific with your bylaws. Decide how you will deal with members who are always late for meetings, what to do about a host who cancels at the last minute, and so on. These problems usually arise when a member is bogged down by too many other commitments or is losing interest in the group. Having as much information in writing about the workings of the group and what is expected of each member leaves little room for errors and misjudgment later. You may want to include in your bylaws such matters as whether a budget needs to be assigned for each dish, or if evening meetings will end

### RECRUITING MEMBERS

When seeking members, here are some things to consider:

For a cooking club focused mainly on socializing and camaraderie, we recommend that you recruit members from already-established social connections: work, a parents' group, your neighborhood, your gym, your community center, school, or church.

For a cooking group that will focus primarily on cooking healthy meals, *Cooking Light* magazine has an active online community message board (www.community.cookinglight.com) organized by location: the West, Midwest, South, Northeast, plus a section for people who live outside of the United States. Participants are encouraged to let people know that they are interested in starting or joining a cooking club in their towns.

For a cooking club that will focus on gourmet cooking, look at the postings on Epicurious.com, Craigslist.org, eGullet.org, Chowhound.com, and Meetup.com. These Web sites offer some of the best community boards that post cooking club information.

at a particular time because some members must be at work early the next morning. Whatever the issue, keeping the lines of communication open is key.

The secretary should also keep a list of the hosting schedule, maintain the group contact list, and keep everyone informed of any changes. In our group, Maria oversees the particulars, and she has kept us ticking like clockwork all these years. She looks after the ebb and flow of the group, and any concerns anyone may have are handled through her. She has held this position since our group was formed; however, you may wish to switch the secretary role every year or two.

We also recommend meeting every six months or so to discuss the club and the bylaws. Regularly ask your group for their ideas for club meetings and events, and for their opinions and feedback on other aspects of the club that they may want to discuss.

## MEMBERSHIP FEES AND COSTS

Consider whether to charge a membership fee to cover food and expenses, and whether the fee will be monthly or annual. While many cooking clubs like to keep things informal with no fee structure at all, other clubs charge fees to cover some or all of the food or entertaining expenses. Some cooking clubs charge a fee that covers the alcoholic beverages served at the gathering, and some charge a monthly fee for the sole purpose of raising money for a predetermined charity, such as a food bank.

## Planning the Menu

This book has twelve eight-course menus organized by theme, just to get you started. But since planning the menu is fun for most self-respecting food geeks, feel free to omit and substitute as much as you like. We know that deciding what to serve at a gathering is almost as much fun as the event itself. It is also a very important process. An uninspired, boring menu will make for a boring evening, as well.

## WHO WILL PLAN THE MENUS?

Menu planning varies widely among cooking clubs. There are several options, but the most popular we've encountered is to have the host plan the menu and assign dishes and recipes to each member of the club. Some other options are for the club to vote on the menu, or simply proceed with no menu at all—the group just decides on a theme and each member chooses a course to prepare with the theme in mind.

Above all, when planning your menus, have fun, and take care when assigning the recipes for each person. Giving the salad course to the same person three months in a row will be a drag, so remember to mix things up. And don't be afraid to challenge each other. Since Michelle had been a pastry chef at one time, at first she was always assigned the dessert course. Wanting to break out of her usual routine, she asked to prepare other courses as well. So although according to our club's rules the host calls the shots and assigns the dishes, we also take special requests into consideration.

## SERVING THE MEAL

Before you plan a menu, consider whether the dishes will be served buffet style or individually plated. Our cooking club prefers to plate our dishes for each member because it helps us practice our presentation skills. The host coordinates the schedule and lets each person know when it is time to head to the kitchen and serve her dish.

When planning a menu, here are some tips we've picked up over the years: Try to alternate heavy and light courses. Start your menu with lighter, more subtle flavors and proceed to more intense, bolder flavors as you go along. Provide plenty of textural contrast by including smooth dishes with crunchy dishes. Provide flavor contrast by including creamy dishes with acidic dishes. Provide dishes with contrasting colors for eye appeal. Finally, if several dishes need to be in the oven just before serving, choose recipes that call for similar oven temperatures. A cohesive menu that flows together like a symphony is what we all strive for.

## WHERE WILL THE COOKING TAKE PLACE?

Consider whether your club will do the cooking together, or whether members will cook at home and finish the dish in the host's kitchen when necessary. If one of the members has a kitchen big enough for the group to cook in together, lucky you! Perhaps you would like to meet at the same location every time. Many cooking clubs prefer to rotate locations, giving everyone an opportunity to host. If space is an issue, how about renting an industrial kitchen at a local culinary school, community center, church, or restaurant? More and more people have access to backyard kitchens, so why not take your love of cooking to the great outdoors? There are many possibilities to consider.

With as many people as we have in our group, we found it best to prepare each of our assigned dishes at home and bring them to the event. Some dishes can be made only up to a certain point at home and must be finished in the host's kitchen; sometimes a quick warm-up in the oven is all that's needed. If your club chooses a similar plan, it is important to choose dishes that will taste as good when reheated and that are easily transported. Ice cream made ahead of time and then carted through town in a hot car is not a good idea.

## LEFTOVERS: IS THERE SUCH A THING AS TOO MUCH?

One of the best rewards of cooking club dinners is the array of delicious foods that remain after the meal. Make sure you plan ahead for your leftovers. Will they be divvied up for all the members after dinner, or will each person take home only the remnants of the dish they prepared? If the former, should members bring to-go containers to the gatherings, or will that be the host's responsibility?

## It's All in the Details

When we originally formed our cooking club, we decided that we wanted each event to be remarkable. We wanted our guests to be excited to come each month, and we wanted our top priorities to be great food, great wine, and great conversation. When you come to an event thrown by any of us, you enter knowing that you are going to have a ball. We've thrown some amazing parties, such as our New Orleans Mardi Gras night, with Spanish moss hanging from the chandeliers and beads thrown around guests' necks as they enter the room. Whether our theme is a Hawaiian luau or a tribute to Greek cuisine, everyone does their best to make each event memorable.

Each month, the host comes up with little touches that make every event fun and tie in to that particular theme.

Now, we are all busy women without much extra time on our hands, but we've learned that going that extra step can take a gathering from being just another dinner party to a bona fide "event," one that we will still be talking about months later. We are not set designers—not one of us is Colin Cowie or Jonathan Adler, and we don't want to be. Going overboard with your theme causes extra stress for the next person who has to host. Remember, you are not entertaining the Queen of England or Martha Stewart. These are your friends, and the food comes first, but don't underestimate the power of a beautiful centerpiece and pleasant lighting, either. We love the little touches that each of us brings to our events, and to help you out, we've included in each chapter some tips and suggestions for ways to make your cooking club event a joy to attend. You'll be surprised at how these little touches add up.

## THEME NIGHTS

Theme events are useful for cooking clubs, especially those focused on learning cooking basics and exploring different cuisines (as opposed to those that are focused on recipe swapping or progressive dinners). Decide how your club will select the themes: will the entire club choose them together, or will it be up to the host? How far do you want to go with themes: will you work the theme into the invitations, décor, and music, or will you keep it to the food only?

## WINE AND COCKTAILS

Many cooking clubs focus on wine as well as food. All the menus in this book include a cocktail recipe, but if your group is interested in wine and beer you might do a tasting evening, or have pairings with each course. In that case, consider setting up a drink budget, or rotate drink responsibilities among the group.

## DISTRIBUTING RECIPES

Consider making photocopies of the recipes prepared and served that evening. Decide who will be responsible for making the copies and assembling the recipe packet to give to members at each cooking club gathering.

## CLEANING UP

Let's face it: no one likes to clean, but at the end of the night, someone's gotta do it. Consider the cleanup responsibilities. Is everyone going to stay after to help? Is the host responsible? Or should you have a cleanup committee?

## COOKING CLUB HISTORY

Make sure to preserve your club's history. Though not key to its survival, this documentation is fun to maintain, and to later use to relive the moments that have made your club special. Keep a digital camera handy and take photos of the people and the dishes served at your gatherings; keep copies of the invitations, the menus, and any other keepsakes or mementos of your cooking club. These will be very helpful if a member should have to move away and you want to prepare a farewell scrapbook or CD-ROM with all your memories together.

## INVITATIONS

Our group enjoys preparing the invitations for each event. These we make lovingly by hand, and we send them by good old U.S. mail, not via e-mail or Evite.com. This takes some time, but to us it is worth it. We appreciate the old-school style and romance of a formal invitation. It sets the tone for the event, and it gets everyone excited for what's to come. We are a creative bunch, and each month a lovely invitation arrives, elaborately decorated, letting us know the month's theme, menu, time, and place. We all look forward to finding them in the mailbox.

Handmade invitations also show the other members just how important the event is to the host. We know of other clubs where members habitually go AWOL or don't take the group very seriously. Our invitations set the bar high, right from the start. Our daily lives can be pretty crazy and hectic, full of those special moments when we find ourselves saying things like,

"Who put the puppy in the laundry hamper again?" or, "What is that stuff dripping from your pockets, and why does it smell like cheese?" Moments such as these are brightened, if only briefly, when a cooking club invitation arrives, beckoning us to a civilized and lovely meal with friends.

Such fun our group has had over the years. We've dined on Moroccan feasts accompanied by a belly dancer; we've made a meal in tribute to all things Anthony Bourdain, featuring a "shrine" of pictures surrounded by candles (as Dina confesses, "I *heart* him"). We have experimented with nearly every known cooking technique; heck, we've even cured our own bacon for a breakfast meeting. ("Everything goes better with bacon" is one of our favorite mottoes, and really, if it wasn't for bacon, would the average person ever care to know what a water chestnut even was?) We've churned our own ice cream, prepared frog legs, rabbit, and turtle, and downed it all with many a perfectly blended cocktail. We've had ourselves a grand old time, all in the name of good food and good company.

# Breakfast is Better with Friends:
## A Little Laughter and Some Egg-citing Conversation

*Breakfast with Friends: Few Things Are Better*
*Cross Your Fingers and Hope for Good Weather*
*Come Enjoy Good Food and Conversation on a*
*Leisurely Sunday Morning*

## Menu

Berry Good Morning Breakfast Spritzer

Sweet Berries and Minted Sugar with Homemade Yogurt

Blueberry-Lemon Muffins with Cinnamon-Sugar Topping

Buttery Orange Scones

Zesty Lemon Curd

Blackberry-Cinnamon Butter

Heavenly Salmon Hash Benedict

Mushroom and Zucchini Puff-Pastry Quiche

# Berry Good Morning Breakfast Spritzer

*This drink reminds us of fellow cooking club member Maria. Both are bubbly, with just the right amount of sweetness! This is a great drink to serve a crowd because you can make the berry puree ahead and keep it in the refrigerator, then mix the spritzers right before serving. Feel free to substitute an Italian Prosecco, Spanish Cava, or a good domestic sparkler for the Champagne.*

Makes 10 spritzers

> 1 cup frozen unsweetened blueberries
> 1 cup frozen unsweetened strawberries
> 4 cups orange juice
> ¼ cup granulated sugar
> 1 bottle (750 ml) chilled Champagne or other sparkling wine
> Fresh mint sprigs for garnish, if desired

Set aside 10 of the best-looking blueberries for the garnish. In a food processor or blender, purée the blueberries and strawberries with 2 tablespoons of the orange juice and the sugar until smooth. Strain the mixture through a fine sieve into a small bowl, discarding the seeds.

Briefly stir the remaining orange juice and Champagne together in a large pitcher. To serve, pour some of the berry purée evenly into 10 champagne flutes and fill with the champagne and orange juice mixture. Garnish each flute with a reserved blueberry and a mint sprig if desired.

# Sweet Berries and Minted Sugar with Homemade Yogurt

*We can remember our moms making homemade yogurt when we were children. We've learned that it is such a simple process and tastes so fresh that it's really the way to go for cooking club. But feel free to substitute your favorite brand of good quality store-bought yogurt. Fresh fruit paired with homemade yogurt is not only good for you, but it also tastes out of this world. The minted sugar is delicious mixed with fruit or used to flavor a cup of hot cocoa. Or try it for decorating the rim of a mojito cocktail glass.*

Makes 8 servings

> ¼ cup fresh mint leaves, loosely packed
> 3 tablespoons sugar
>
> ---
>
> 1 cup fresh blackberries
> 2 cups fresh strawberries, hulls removed, and cut in half
> 1 cup fresh blueberries
> Zest of 1 small lime (about 1 teaspoon)
> 2 cups Homemade Yogurt (recipe follows) or good-quality
>    plain store-bought yogurt

Pulse the mint and sugar together in a food processor until well incorporated. Store the sugar in the refrigerator until just before serving.

Put the blackberries, strawberries, and blueberries in a large bowl, and sprinkle the minted sugar and lime zest over them. Stir gently to combine. Spoon ½ cup of yogurt into each serving dish. Serve the berries alongside or on top of each serving of yogurt.

## Homemade Yogurt

Makes eight ½-cup servings

> 4 cups whole milk
> ⅓ cup powdered milk (optional)
> 2 tablespoons plain, unsweetened, natural yogurt with active yogurt cultures

Over medium-high heat, in a medium-size heavy-bottomed saucepan, warm the milk with the powdered milk, if using, and whisk until well combined. Clip a candy thermometer to the side of the saucepan and make sure that the tip is resting in the milk but is not in contact with the bottom of the pan. Stirring constantly, bring the milk to 180°F, then remove from the heat and allow it to cool to 115°F. Once the milk reaches 115°F, add the yogurt and mix well to combine.

Transfer the mixture to a clean bowl and cover tightly with plastic wrap. Wrap the bowl well with a heavy towel or a blanket. Set the bowl aside in a cool oven with the door closed for 6 to 8 hours, or longer, according to your taste. The yogurt will get tangier the longer it sits.

Store the yogurt in a sealed container in the refrigerator, and allow it to cool completely before serving. It will thicken somewhat as it chills. Put a few tablespoons of yogurt in a covered container to use as the starter for your next batch. The starter can be kept in the refrigerator for up to two weeks.

## HOW TO MAKE YOGURT

There are a few pointers for making homemade yogurt, but the process is a lot easier than you may think. Yogurt is basically scalded milk that is allowed to ferment with an added yogurt starter containing live yogurt cultures. Any kind of good-quality plain, unsweetened, natural yogurt will make a fine starter for this recipe, as long as it contains active yogurt cultures. Look for a brand that contains only milk (and possibly cream), and the live, active yogurt cultures. Avoid any that contain sweeteners, flavorings, cornstarch, gums, carrageenan, or other thickeners.

Scalding the milk kills the bad bacteria that cause milk to turn sour, and the yogurt starter introduces the good bacteria (the live cultures) that "culture" the milk and turn it into yogurt. All you really need to make yogurt is a candy thermometer to make sure that the milk reaches the correct temperature, and a warm place to keep the milk where it can ferment.

This particular recipe uses cow's milk, but if you can get your hands on some goat's or sheep's milk, lucky you! Any kind will work, whether it is full fat, 2 percent or 1 percent fat, but do make sure that the milk contains lactose. Lactose-free milk does not contain the sugar necessary for the yogurt to ferment properly. The longer it ferments, the more tangy it will become, and the more active yogurt cultures it will produce.

You can make the yogurt with or without adding powdered milk, but using it will make your yogurt thicker and you can use non-fat or full fat varieties. For extra-thick Greek-style yogurt, you can simply strain the finished yogurt through a fine sieve or paper coffee filter, over a bowl to catch the drips, in the refrigerator for several hours or overnight.

*All happiness depends on a leisurely breakfast.*
—John Gunther

## Tips for Entertaining
## at Breakfast

- Attach your printed breakfast invitation to a small bottle of real maple syrup, or a small bag of fresh coffee or tea, and hand-deliver to each guest.

- No breakfast would be complete without lots of fresh, hot coffee. Set up a serve-yourself coffee station in an easily accessible place for your guests, and provide an assortment of sugars, creamers, and milk.

- Create special party favors by canning your own jellies or jams, and wrap the jars with a decorative bow.

- Nothing says breakfast like oranges. Arrange them along the table, on your kitchen counter, or wherever your guests will gather. For an eye-opening centerpiece, fill a clear, heavy vase with oranges, add water, and top off with fresh-cut flowers.

- Invite your guests to wear their craziest pajamas for a contest, and then vote on them. The winner receives a gift certificate to a local breakfast joint or coffee house.

# Blueberry-Lemon Muffins with Cinnamon-Sugar Topping

*Michelle is a muffin gal through and through. When Elaine of* Seinfeld *fame wanted to open a shop that sold only muffin tops, she could totally relate. Heck, she would have kept that shop in business! These muffins rise up into beautiful golden crowns. The cinnamon-sugar topping makes them irresistible, and the yogurt lends a flavorful tang that your cooking club will love. Don't use muffin-pan liners with this recipe or the muffins won't puff up as much.*

Makes 12 muffins

3 cups plus 1 tablespoon all-purpose flour
1 tablespoon baking powder
½ teaspoon baking soda
¼ pound (1 stick) plus 2 tablespoons unsalted butter, softened
¾ cup sugar
Zest of 2 small lemons (about 2 teaspoons)
2 large eggs
1½ cups plain low-fat yogurt
1 cup blueberries
Nonstick cooking spray

1 teaspoon ground cinnamon
¼ cup sugar

Preheat the oven to 375°F.

In a large bowl, mix together the 3 cups of flour, baking powder, and baking soda. Set aside.

In the bowl of a standing mixer fitted with the paddle attachment, cream together ¼ pound of the butter, sugar, and lemon zest on medium speed until light and fluffy, about 2 minutes. Add the eggs 1 at a time, beating well after each addition. With the mixer on low speed, add the flour mixture and the yogurt alternately, a little at a time, until just blended.

Put the blueberries in a medium-size bowl and sprinkle them with the remaining tablespoon of flour. Mix very gently, then gently stir the berries into the batter.

Spray a 12-cup muffin pan liberally with the cooking spray and divide the batter evenly among the 12 cups. Bake the muffins for 25 to 30 minutes, or until the muffin tops are lightly golden brown. Immediately remove the muffins from the pan and allow them to cool slightly.

To make the topping, mix the cinnamon and sugar together in a small bowl. Put the remaining 2 tablespoons of butter in another bowl large enough to fit a muffin top and microwave for 10 seconds or until melted. While the muffins are still warm, dip the muffin tops in the melted butter, then roll them in the cinnamon sugar. Serve warm.

# Buttery Orange Scones

*Homemade scones are a special treat perfect for a leisurely breakfast spent with good friends. The secret to perfect scones is to work as quickly as possible when mixing the ingredients, then put the scones into the preheated oven right away. Serve these scones hot from the oven with the Zesty Lemon Curd on page 8 and the Blackberry-Cinnamon Butter on page 9 alongside.*

Makes twelve 3-inch scones

> 4 cups all-purpose flour
> 1 tablespoon baking powder
> 3 tablespoons sugar
> 1½ teaspoons salt
> ¼ pound (1 stick) unsalted butter, chilled and cut into ½-inch pieces
> Zest of 1 to 2 oranges (about 1 tablespoon)
> 1¾ cups whole milk
> 1 egg white, beaten until smooth

Preheat the oven to 450°F.

Sift together the flour, baking powder, sugar, and salt into a large bowl. Cut the butter into the flour mixture with a fork or a pastry cutter until the flour resembles coarse meal, leaving a few larger lumps of butter.

In a small bowl, stir together the orange zest and the milk. Working quickly, blend the wet and dry ingredients together with a rubber spatula until just combined. The dough should be soft and slightly wet.

Turn the dough out onto a well-floured work surface, and pat it out to a thickness of ¾ inch. Cut the dough into rounds using a greased and floured 3-inch biscuit cutter. Between cuts, dip the cutter in flour as needed to prevent sticking. If desired, you can cut the dough into triangle shapes instead.

Place the rounds or triangles on a lightly greased baking sheet, about 1½ inches apart. Using a pastry brush, brush each scone with a small amount of the egg white. Bake the scones for 15 minutes, or until golden brown.

# Zesty Lemon Curd

*Lemon curd will keep in the refrigerator for up to a month; we encourage you to make a double batch and use it to slather on just about anything you can think of. It makes a delicious filling for individual tarts and cupcakes, as well.*

Makes 1½ cups

> 1 egg
> 3 egg yolks
> Zest of 2 large lemons (about 2 tablespoons)
> ½ cup freshly squeezed lemon juice (about 3 lemons)
> 1 cup sugar
> 6 tablespoons unsalted butter, cut into ½-inch cubes

In a medium-size bowl, beat together the egg and the egg yolks, and set aside.

Heat the lemon zest, lemon juice, and sugar over medium heat in a small, heavy-bottomed pot. When the sugar has completely dissolved, after about 3 minutes, take the pot off the heat and whisk in the egg mixture a little at a time, until it is fully incorporated.

Put the pot back on the stove over low heat, and add the butter, a little at a time, whisking well after each addition. Continue to cook the mixture over low heat, stirring constantly for 6 minutes, or until the mixture thickens enough to coat the back of the spoon.

Strain the lemon curd through a fine-mesh sieve into a sterilized glass bowl and cover with plastic wrap. Put the lemon curd in the refrigerator until ready to serve. The lemon curd will thicken more as it chills.

# Blackberry-Cinnamon Butter

*In the late spring, blackberries grow wild all over our neighborhood. In the evening, Michelle's family loves to take walks along a nearby bike path, picking blackberries along the way. Most of them are eaten before Michelle returns home, but all she needs is a handful of berries to make this special blackberry butter.*

Makes about 1 cup

> ½ cup fresh ripe blackberries
> ¼ cup sugar
> 1 teaspoon ground cinnamon
> 2 tablespoons water
> ¼ pound (1 stick) unsalted butter, softened

Over high heat, in a heavy-bottomed saucepan, combine the berries, sugar, cinnamon, and water and bring them just to a boil. Lightly crush the berries with the back of a spoon or with a fork. Reduce the heat to medium-low and simmer, stirring constantly, for 4 or 5 minutes, until the berries have softened and the juices have thickened slightly.

Remove the pan from the heat and allow the mixture to cool for 5 minutes, or until cool to the touch. Put the pan in the refrigerator for 10 minutes to allow the mixture to become syrupy and thicken even more.

Put the berries and the butter in a medium-size bowl. Using an electric mixer, beat the softened butter and the berries together until just combined. Put the butter in a small ramekin or crock, cover with plastic wrap, and keep in the refrigerator until ready to use. The butter will keep in the refrigerator for up to one week. Allow the butter to soften slightly at room temperature before serving.

# Heavenly Salmon Hash Benedict

*This dish was inspired by Michelle's mom, Sherry, who warns that the recipe can be a little tricky to bring everything together and serve warm. The best approach is to make the salmon hash and the hollandaise sauce up to an hour in advance, then poach the eggs. When the water for the eggs has just reached a simmer, and you have slid the last egg in the water, put the hash in a preheated 325°F oven, and set the prepared hollandaise sauce, in a saucepan, over low heat. Heat both the hash and the sauce for about 5 to 7 minutes. To serve, transfer the hash to a serving platter and top it with the eggs and then the hollandaise sauce.*

Makes 8 servings

> 1 pound precooked medium-rare salmon
> 3 tablespoons freshly squeezed lemon juice (about 1 lemon)
> 4 cups cold water
> 5 medium-size russet potatoes
> 6 tablespoons plus 1 tablespoon plus 1 tablespoon unsalted butter
> 1 large red bell pepper, finely chopped
> 1 large yellow bell pepper, finely chopped
> 1 large yellow onion, diced
> 1 tablespoon minced fresh dill
> 1 tablespoon minced fresh parsley
> 1 teaspoon salt
> 1 teaspoon freshly ground black pepper
> Hollandaise Sauce (recipe follows)
> Perfectly Poached Eggs (recipe follows)

Combine the lemon juice and the water in a large bowl. Wash and peel the potatoes. Shred the potatoes through the large holes of a box grater into the lemon water. Keeping the potatoes in the lemon water until ready to use will prevent them from turning brown. When you are ready to proceed, drain the shredded potatoes and wrap them in a clean kitchen towel, squeezing to remove the excess liquid.

In a large nonstick skillet, heat 6 tablespoons of the butter over medium-high heat until it just starts to smoke. Very carefully, place all the potatoes in the skillet, pressing them down into a thick pancake, and allow them to brown. Do not try to turn the potatoes until they have started to brown around the edges, about 10 minutes. Lower the heat to medium and continue cooking and stirring until potatoes are golden brown, about 20 minutes. Remove the potatoes and drain them well on paper towels. Keep warm.

Add a tablespoon of butter to the skillet, then add the red and yellow peppers and the onion, and sauté until the vegetables are soft. Stir in the dill, parsley, salt, and pepper. Transfer to a shallow dish and keep warm.

Wipe out the skillet with a paper towel and melt the remaining tablespoon of butter over medium heat. When the butter has melted, add the precooked salmon to reheat it and chop it into bite-size pieces with a spatula. The salmon will take only about 1 minute. Return the potatoes and vegetables to the pan and stir carefully to combine.

Serve the hash topped with a poached egg and drizzled with hollandaise sauce.

## Hollandaise Sauce
Makes 1 cup or enough for 8 servings

> 3 egg yolks
> 2 tablespoons boiling water
> ¼ pound (1 stick) unsalted butter, melted
> ¼ cup freshly squeezed lemon juice (about 1½ lemons)
> ½ teaspoon salt
> ¼ teaspoon freshly ground black pepper
> Dash of cayenne pepper, to taste
> 2 teaspoons fresh dill, minced

Put the eggs in a blender jar or the bowl of a food processor fitted with a steel blade. If using a blender, set it to low speed. Slowly add the water, then add the butter in a slow, thin stream. Add the lemon juice, salt, pepper, cayenne, and dill, and quickly pulse just to combine. Place hollandaise sauce in a small saucepan set over low heat, and allow the mixture to thicken slightly, for about 3 minutes. Keep the sauce warm until ready to serve if using immediately, or store, tightly covered, in the refrigerator [for up to 3 days], then warm over low heat for 2 to 3 minutes before serving.

## Perfectly Poached Eggs

Makes 8 servings

> Water for poaching
> ½ teaspoon salt
> 2 teaspoons white vinegar
> 8 very fresh large eggs

Fill a large skillet with 1 inch of water and add the salt and the vinegar. Bring water to a very gentle simmer.

Carefully break each egg into individual small cups or bowls, and gently slide them, one after the other, into the barely simmering water from the side of the pan. If the eggs start to overcrowd each other, poach the eggs in 2 batches. Let the eggs poach for 3½ minutes, or until the eggs are slightly underdone.

Remove the eggs from the water with a slotted spoon, one at a time. Hold each egg above the water and allow the water to drain from the spoon. Carefully place the eggs in a serving dish large enough to hold them without crowding. Do not discard water. Just before serving, carefully dunk each egg in hot water to finish and warm.

# Mushroom and Zucchini Puff-Pastry Quiche

*When this quiche was served at cooking club, there wasn't one piece left afterward. This is less time consuming to make than a regular quiche, and we think it tastes better—after all, it's puff pastry! Don't worry if the filling oozes over the sides. The borders will puff up nicely and hold everything in place.*

Makes 8 servings

> 2 sheets (one 17.3-ounce package) frozen puff pastry, thawed according to package directions
> 2 tablespoons unsalted butter
> 1 cup sliced mushrooms
> ½ teaspoon plus ½ teaspoon salt
> ½ teaspoon plus ½ teaspoon pepper
> 1 cup diced zucchini
> ½ cup thinly sliced yellow bell pepper
> ½ cup thinly sliced red bell pepper
> 2 cups coarsely grated Swiss cheese
>
> _____
>
> 2 eggs
> 1 tablespoon chopped fresh rosemary
> ¼ teaspoon grated nutmeg
> 1 cup sour cream
> 2 cloves garlic, minced

Preheat the oven to 400°F.

Carefully unfold a pastry sheet onto each of 2 rimmed baking sheets and set aside.

Melt the butter in a medium-size skillet over medium heat. Add the mushrooms, ½ teaspoon of the salt, and ½ teaspoon of the pepper, and sauté the mushrooms until they just begin to brown, about 4 minutes. Add the zucchini and the bell peppers; cook, stirring, until just heated through, about 1 minute, and remove from the heat.

Spread the vegetable mixture evenly over each of the puff pastry sheets, leaving a ½-inch plain border on all sides. Sprinkle evenly with the cheese.

In a small bowl, whisk together the eggs, rosemary, the remaining salt and pepper, and nutmeg. Add the sour cream and garlic and mix until well blended. Spoon the egg mixture over the vegetables and cheese, smooth it over evenly, and bake until puffed and golden brown, about 30 to 35 minutes. Cool slightly before slicing. Cut each pastry into 4 pieces and serve.

# The Newport Gourmet Club

It was their involvement in their community that was the catalyst for Ken and Nancy Stevens becoming members of the Newport Gourmet Club in Newport, Oregon. At a fundraising auction for the Samaritan Pacific Communities Hospital, Ken and Nancy donated an Italian dinner for six. It was there that they met their future cooking club members.

As luck would have it, the winning bidders of the donated Italian dinner were current members of the Newport Gourmet Club. "I was so nervous to make that meal for them," says Nancy. "When I learned that the people I was preparing the meal for were all members of a cooking club, I felt a lot of anxiety. To make matters worse, they told me they might let me and Ken join the club if the dinner was good enough. They were joking of course, but talk about pressure!" Nancy needn't have worried. Her Italian dinner was a huge success; she and Ken were invited to join the group and they have been members ever since.

The Newport Gourmet Club, which has been going strong since 2001, consists of five married couples in their fifties and beyond who all share a love of cooking and entertaining. The group meets every other month, and they stay organized by getting together once a year to review their calendars and set the meeting dates for the year ahead. For their events, the host will plan the entire menu and make the main dish, and the other dishes served that night are assigned to the rest of the group.

When asked if the men are as accomplished in the kitchen as the women, Nancy says with a laugh, "Oh, absolutely. In some cases, the men are better cooks than the women of the group. The men love to get behind the barbecue for the summer cookouts, and they don't mind getting in there and getting their hands dirty." Nancy mentions how much the men love the social aspect of their gatherings. "When we were possibly going to have to move a gourmet club meeting back a month, my husband was concerned it would be too long between meetings. He was missing seeing his friends."

Over the years, the group's members have formed deep bonds with each other. They socialize outside of the club, go to tailgating events together, and some even take vacations together. These bonds were never more evident than when the parent of one of the members died. The entire cooking club banded together in support and helped to prepare all the food that was served after the funeral. "I was so proud of all of us in that moment, and I marveled at how much we all care for each other," says Nancy.

While this group certainly enjoys the friendships that have developed, the food is the star attraction. A Mardi Gras theme was a huge success, as was a menu planned around lemons. "Lemons were incorporated into every dish, and the entire house was decked out in colorful lemon yellows, from the table centerpiece to the linens and place settings. It was just beautiful," says Nancy.

Fun is a priority for this group as well. "We love being silly," says Nancy. At one event, "while the host was tending to a roast in the oven, the rest of the group was in the living room, socializing. We were a little puzzled when we saw the host tiptoeing into the living room with her fingers on her lips. The next thing we knew, she was telling us to be quiet because the meat was resting. Well, we all busted up laughing over that one." At another gathering, the group was dining on lobster tails under the stars. "This was a pretty fancy event," says Nancy. "There were flickering white lights placed in the surrounding trees and even under the dining table, and there was classical music playing softly in the background. I forget who it was, but one of the husbands asked if we could turn off the classical music and put on the Oregon State Beavers football game." She adds, "Since most of the members of the cooking club are alumni of Oregon State University, it seemed like a perfectly logical request."

Ken and Nancy Stevens are both so happy to be involved with such a warm and supportive group of food lovers, and they believe that cooking together as couples has strengthened the bonds of their friendships as well as the bonds within their marriages. "If you can cook together, you can do anything together," says Nancy. We couldn't agree more.

*Laissez les Bons Temps Rouler!*
*It's Time to Let the Good Times Roll, Mardi Gras Style*
*There Will Be Plenty of Beads—Enough for All*
*So Come One, Come All, We'll Have a Ball!*

## Menu

Hurricane Cocktail

Hush Puppies

Salad of Crabmeat-Stuffed Artichokes with a Tabasco Dipping Sauce

Falling-off-the-Bone Chicken Étouffée

Cheesy Baked Grits

Spicy Collard Greens

Chocolate-Pecan Bread Pudding with Warm Bourbon Sauce

Cinnamon Café au Lait with Spiced Whipped Cream

# Hurricane Cocktail

*For the past couple of years in the spring, we have traveled to New Orleans with our husbands for the French Quarter Festival. There is nothing better than listening to great zydeco music while eating crawfish and drinking a hurricane (or three) with good friends. Our cooking club loved these, and for those who had never been to the Big Easy, they felt as if they were right there on Bourbon Street. If you can't find passion-fruit juice, mango juice makes a nice substitute.*

Makes 1 cocktail

> 3 ounces dark rum
> ¼ cup orange juice
> 2 teaspoons freshly squeezed lime juice (about ¼ lime)
> ¼ cup passion-fruit juice
> 1 tablespoon simple syrup
> 1 tablespoon grenadine syrup
> Maraschino cherries and orange slices for garnish

Mix the rum, orange juice, lime juice, passion-fruit juice, and simple syrup in a cocktail shaker; add the grenadine and some ice. Shake until thoroughly combined. Strain the mixture over ice cubes into a highball or hurricane glass and garnish with a cherry and an orange slice.

# Hush Puppies

*Hush puppies are a southern staple, and no tribute to New Orleans would be complete without them. Make sure that your baking powder is fresh so you don't end up with little balls of lead. These are easy to make and taste amazing. A hurricane cocktail in one hand and a hush puppy in the other—is there anything better? Blast the zydeco music and you've got yourself a party.*

Makes 24 hush puppies or enough for 8 servings

1½ cups yellow cornmeal
½ cup all-purpose flour
2 teaspoons baking powder
2 teaspoons salt
1 teaspoon sugar
¼ teaspoon hot red pepper flakes
¼ cup grated onion
1 jalapeño pepper, stemmed, seeded, and minced
1 cup buttermilk
1 egg
6 cups vegetable oil

Put the cornmeal, flour, baking powder, salt, sugar, red pepper flakes, onion, and jalapeño in a medium-size bowl and mix thoroughly. Whisk together the buttermilk and the egg. Add the milk mixture to the cornmeal mixture and stir until well blended.

Fill a large, heavy cast-iron skillet with 1 inch of oil. Heat the oil until the temperature reaches 350°F. Working in small batches of about 5 or 6, add 1 tablespoon of batter at a time to the hot oil and fry for 2 to 3 minutes, or until the hush puppies are a nice golden brown. Drain the hush puppies on paper towels and serve hot.

# Salad of Crabmeat-Stuffed Artichokes with a Tabasco Dipping Sauce

*A well-prepared stuffed artichoke is a terrific way to showcase fresh jumbo lump crabmeat and makes for a beautiful presentation that your guests will surely appreciate. Cut the artichoke stem flush with the base of the artichoke so that it will sit upright on the plate without tipping over. You don't want to lose a morsel of that precious crabmeat. Every component of this salad can be prepared and assembled in advance, making it ideal for your cooking club.*

Makes 8 servings

> 8 medium-size artichokes
> ½ cup minced celery
> 2 shallots, minced
> 2 cloves garlic, minced
> 4 tablespoons minced green bell pepper
> 3 tablespoons freshly squeezed lemon juice (about 1 lemon)
> 3 tablespoons extra-virgin olive oil
> 2 tablespoons capers, rinsed, plus more for garnish, if desired
> 1 teaspoon salt
> ¼ teaspoon freshly ground black pepper
> ¼ teaspoon paprika
> 1 pound fresh jumbo lump crabmeat, picked over for any bits of shell
> Tabasco Dipping Sauce (recipe follows)

To prepare the artichokes, cut the stem flush with the base, and cut off the tight top leaves to remove the prickly tips. With a pair of scissors, trim each side leaf to remove the prickles.

Put the artichokes in a large pot of boiling salted water. If they do not fit easily, use 2 pots. Boil the artichokes for 25 to 40 minutes, making sure that they do not overcook. The artichoke is done when the outer leaves pull out easily. Drain the artichokes upside down. When cool, press the leaves back gently, and pull out the small, undeveloped white leaves from the center. Scrape out the choke with a small spoon. Let the artichokes chill in the refrigerator until ready to use.

In medium-size bowl, mix together the celery, shallots, garlic, green pepper, lemon juice, oil, capers, salt, black pepper, and paprika. Very gently, stir in the crabmeat, trying not to break up the lumps of crabmeat. Divide the crabmeat into 8 portions, and heap some of the mixture inside each of the cooked artichokes. Garnish with a few more capers if desired. Serve with the Tabasco Dipping Sauce.

## Tabasco Dipping Sauce
Makes 2 cups or enough for 8 servings

> 2 cups mayonnaise
> 4 tablespoons freshly squeezed lemon juice (about 1⅓ lemon)
> Tabasco sauce

Put the mayonnaise and lemon juice in a small bowl. Add the Tabasco sauce to taste, and stir to combine. Pass the dipping sauce at the table.

# Falling-off-the-Bone Chicken Étouffée

*Étouffée is the French word meaning "smothered." We can't think of anything better than the grits that accompany this recipe, smothered in the delicious sauce. Most recipes for étouffée feature seafood. This one is made with chicken, which just melts in your mouth, and we don't think you will miss the seafood one little bit. For your cooking club, you can make this a day ahead and reheat it once you arrive at the host's. In fact, this dish tastes even better when prepared a day in advance.*

Makes 8 servings

16 skin-on chicken thighs (about 5 pounds)
2½ teaspoons salt
1 teaspoon freshly ground black pepper
1 teaspoon cayenne pepper
5 tablespoons unsalted butter
2 large yellow onions, finely chopped
4 carrots, peeled and finely chopped
4 celery stalks, finely chopped
3 small green bell peppers, finely chopped
8 garlic cloves, minced
6 sprigs fresh thyme
2 bay leaves
1 cup full-bodied red wine, such as Bordeaux or Cabernet Sauvignon
2 cups chicken broth
2 cups canned, crushed tomatoes
½ cup cornstarch
½ cup cold water

Preheat the oven to 350°F.

Remove any excess fat from the chicken thighs, and dry them well with a paper towel. Rub the thighs with salt, pepper, and cayenne. Melt the butter in a large ovenproof pot with a tight-fitting lid over medium heat. Add the chicken thighs to the pot and sauté them in batches until the skin is lightly browned on all sides, about 10 minutes per batch. Do not overcrowd the chicken pieces while browning. Transfer the browned chicken to a large bowl. Do not pour off the fat from the pot.

Put the onions, carrots, celery, and bell peppers in the pot, and sauté them over medium heat until they begin to brown, about 8 minutes. Add the garlic, thyme, and bay leaves, and stir to combine. Put the chicken thighs back in the pot, and stir in the wine, chicken broth, and tomatoes. Bring to a boil over high heat and boil for 5 minutes.

Put the lid on the pot and transfer it to the preheated oven. Cook until the chicken is very tender, about 1 hour and 30 minutes. Remove the pot from the oven, allow it to come to room temperature, and put it in the refrigerator overnight.

The next day, skim the fat from the surface of the étouffée with a large spoon. Reheat the étouffée over medium heat. Carefully remove the chicken thighs from the pot and transfer them to a large bowl. Put the cornstarch and water in a small container with a lid and shake vigorously until there are no lumps. Slowly add the cornstarch mixture to the pot a little at a time, whisking as you do so, until the sauce reaches the desired consistency; you may not need to use all of the cornstarch mixture.

Carefully return the chicken thighs to the pot and let them simmer for about 10 minutes. Remove the bay leaves, adjust the seasoning with salt and pepper to taste, and serve.

# Cheesy Baked Grits

*This recipe is dedicated to Michelle's wonderful grandmother, Patricia Everly. She is from the South, and grits were a staple in her kitchen. It is because of her that Michelle loves grits as much as she does. Not until she was older did Michelle realize that not everyone grew up eating grits, and many in our cooking club had never tried them. If you like polenta, you'll love grits. Try these flavorful, cheesy grits; their creamy texture is so satisfying.*

Makes 8 servings

Unsalted butter for preparing baking dish
4 cups chicken broth
¼ pound (1 stick) unsalted butter
1 teaspoon salt
1 cup stone-ground grits
1 cup coarsely grated extra-sharp cheddar cheese
1 cup coarsely grated Havarti cheese
2 cloves garlic, minced
½ teaspoon cayenne pepper
¾ cup whole milk
2 large eggs

Preheat the oven to 350°F.

Butter an 8- by 8- by 2-inch glass baking dish and set aside.

In a heavy medium-size saucepan, bring the chicken broth, butter, and salt to a boil. Gradually whisk in the grits and reduce the heat to medium. Cook the mixture for about 10 minutes. Remove the grits from the heat and add the cheeses, garlic, and cayenne pepper; stir until cheese is melted.

In a separate bowl, whisk together the milk and eggs. Gradually whisk the egg mixture into the grits until combined. Pour the grits into the prepared baking dish; bake until they are firm in the center and the edges are brown and crispy, about 1 hour and 15 minutes; and serve.

# Spicy Collard Greens

*Fellow cooking club member Nicole may be our newest member, but she seems like she has always been a part of this group. She is a gal that really loves her veggies, and we dedicate this recipe to her. These greens pack a punch, so if you don't care for as much heat, you can cut back on the amount of red pepper flakes. It always surprises us how long it takes to wash and rinse greens, but the time it takes is definitely worth it. Make sure to wash and rinse thoroughly; a mouthful of sand is a no-no!*

Makes 8 servings

½ pound thick-cut pepper bacon, each slice cut into fourths
1 large yellow onion, coarsely chopped
1 cup chicken broth
¼ cup balsamic vinegar
2 tablespoons sugar
1 tablespoon soy sauce
4 cloves garlic, thinly sliced
1 teaspoon salt
¼ teaspoon freshly ground pepper
½ teaspoon hot red pepper flakes
3 pounds collard greens, cleaned well, stems and ribs removed,
    coarsely chopped
Zest of 1 large lemon (about 2 teaspoons)
Tabasco sauce (optional)

Cook the bacon in 2 batches over medium heat until browned in a large, heavy pot or Dutch oven. Drain the bacon on paper towels. Pour off all but 4 tablespoons of the bacon fat from the pot. Sauté the onion until softened and browned slightly, about 5 minutes. Transfer the onions to a bowl.

Put the chicken broth, vinegar, sugar, soy sauce, garlic, salt, pepper, red pepper flakes, and half of the bacon in the pot and cook over medium heat. Stir until the sugar is dissolved. Add half of the greens, tossing until they are slightly wilted. Add the remaining greens and simmer, covered, for 30 minutes. Stir in the onions and simmer, covered, for another 30 minutes, or until the greens are very tender. Top the greens with the lemon zest and remaining bacon and serve. Pass the Tabasco sauce at the table for those who would like their greens even spicier.

# Chocolate-Pecan Bread Pudding
# with Warm Bourbon Sauce

*This recipe has all the elements necessary for a great dessert. It's creamy, it's gooey, and it's simply delicious. This sumptuous dessert is best served warm so that the bourbon sauce can melt into the bread pudding.*

Makes 8 servings

> Unsalted butter for preparing baking dish
> 5 large eggs
> 4 cups whole milk
> ½ cup sugar
> 2½ teaspoons pure vanilla extract
> 2 teaspoons ground cinnamon
> 1 teaspoon grated nutmeg
> ¼ teaspoon salt
> 1-pound loaf day-old French bread, crusts trimmed, cut into 1-inch cubes
> 4 ounces semisweet chocolate, coarsely chopped
> ¼ cup finely chopped toasted pecans
> Warm Bourbon Sauce (recipe follows)

Butter an 8- by 8-inch square baking dish and set aside.

Whisk the eggs together in a large bowl. Stir the milk, sugar, vanilla, cinnamon, nutmeg, and salt together in a medium-size saucepan, and bring the mixture just to a boil over medium heat. Allow it to cool slightly, then gradually pour the milk mixture into the eggs a little at a time, whisking constantly, being careful not to curdle the eggs.

Preheat the oven to 375°F.

To the custard mixture, add the cubed bread, chocolate pieces, and pecans, and stir until combined. Pour the mixture into the prepared baking dish. Stir the bread so that the custard will settle evenly in the pan. Cover the dish tightly with aluminum foil and set it aside for 15 to 20 minutes. While the pudding is resting, bring 3 or 4 cups of water to a boil.

Place the baking dish inside a 13- by 9- by 2-inch baking pan and carefully pour enough boiling water into the pan to come 1 inch up the sides of the pan. Bake until the pudding is golden brown and puffed, about 50 minutes. Serve the bread pudding topped with Warm Bourbon Sauce.

## Warm Bourbon Sauce

Makes 1½ cups or enough for 8 servings

> ½ stick (4 tablespoons) unsalted butter
> ¾ cup sugar
> 5 tablespoons heavy whipping cream
> 3 tablespoons bourbon
> 2 teaspoons freshly squeezed lemon juice (about ⅓ lemon)
> ¼ teaspoon ground cinnamon

Melt the butter over medium heat in a small saucepan. Stir in the sugar, cream, bourbon, lemon juice, and cinnamon, and simmer until thickened and the sugar has melted, about 5 minutes. Serve warm.

*New Orleans food is as delicious as the less criminal forms of sin.*
—Mark Twain

## Tips for a Successful "Big Easy" Party

- Feathered masks (you can purchase these at party stores or online) make great favors for your guests to wear at the party, or you can arrange them as a decorative centerpiece.

- Give strings of Mardi Gras beads to your guests as you greet them, or decorate with them, draping them around plants and chandeliers.

- Hang mock street signs around the room that say "Bourbon Street" or "French Quarter."

- Spanish moss can be bought at any florist's shop. Hang the moss in clumps from the ceiling, large potted plants, and lighting fixtures. Have fun with this, and make it look just like the bayou!

- Display some musical instruments, borrowed or your own, as a centerpiece.

- Purple and gold are the colors of Mardi Gras, so use those colors for your table and centerpieces.

- Fill large hurricane-candle holders with an assortment of beads.

- Zydeco, Cajun, Dixieland, jazz, and blues are ideal music choices. Find some music with a snappy beat to greet your guests as they arrive.

- Attach notes with your guests' names to miniature bottles of Tabasco sauce, or even little harmonicas, and use these as place cards at the table.

# Cinnamon Café au Lait
# with Spiced Whipped Cream

*This is our own tribute to the legendary Café du Monde in New Orleans and their wonderful café au lait, served 24 hours a day, 365 days a year. This recipe has a bit of delicious spice added to the coffee. For our cooking club, we served the traditional coffee blended with chicory to keep it authentic, but any good strong coffee will work. You can also use decaffeinated coffee if your guests prefer.*

Makes 8 servings

3 cups low-fat milk

5 cinnamon sticks

15 whole cloves

8 cups strong chicory coffee, freshly brewed

3 tablespoons plus 1 tablespoon sugar

2 teaspoons plus 1 teaspoon pure vanilla extract

½ cup very cold heavy whipping cream

¼ teaspoon grated nutmeg

Bring the milk, cinnamon sticks, and cloves to a simmer in a small saucepan over medium heat. Remove the pan from the heat and allow the milk mixture to steep for 15 minutes. Strain the mixture, discarding the spices, and bring it back to a simmer. Add the brewed coffee, 3 tablespoons of the sugar, and 2 teaspoons of the vanilla extract, and stir over medium-low heat until the sugar melts and the flavors are blended, about 5 minutes.

Meanwhile, beat the cream, nutmeg, the remaining tablespoon of sugar, and the remaining teaspoon of vanilla in a medium-size bowl, just until soft peaks form.

Pour the hot coffee into heated mugs and add a dollop of the spiced whipped cream. Garnish with more nutmeg if desired.

# Beyond Black-Eyed Peas

Located in Panama City Beach, Florida, the ten eclectic women who make up Beyond Black-Eyed Peas are all members of the Bay Point Women's Club, a local community-building group. It was through their involvement with the Women's Club that they came together to form a club.

They call themselves "Beyond Black-Eyed Peas" and have been meeting since the fall of 2005. "We wanted a name that personified a typical southern food like the black-eyed pea, but would let everyone know that we were about so much more than fried foods and okra," said cooking club member Courtney Hanahan.

The makeup of this group is certainly "beyond" the ordinary. "What a diverse group we are," says cooking club member Carol Proctor. Members range from a retired bank executive from Missouri, a retired school administrator from California, a mother of nine, an owner of a scrap metal business, several retirees, a school teacher–turned decorator and wedding planner, "and then there is the young sexy one that doesn't like to cook, " says Proctor.

They meet the third Tuesday of every month without fail, and for this group it is about the experience as a whole, as well as attention to detail. "In the beginning, the group started out where every member picked a theme and everyone else brought an assigned side dish," said Proctor. "But then we decided that we cooked so much through our involvement with the Bay Point Women's Club, that it would be a treat to have each member cook and entertain us. So now the hostess provides every-thing."

"You have much more control in how each dish is presented when one person does everything," adds Hanahan.

It is up to the host to choose the theme for her dinner. The host is responsible for the appetizer, the main dish, the side dishes, as well as alcohol and dessert. When asked how best to describe the group, Hanahan says with a laugh, "We're all just so cute and fun." While this group may be cute and fun, they can certainly add innova-tive to their list of attributes as well.

"We've had some really creative cooking club events over the years," said Hanahan, who is particularly proud of a theme that she hosted called "Illusions." "Nothing was as it seemed on the surface," she said. The guests were first greeted with a cham-pagne flute filled with white cranberry juice and vodka. The glass had Nerd candies at the bottom for rocks, and was garnished with a gummy fish for an "aquarium" effect. The appetizer was called "Green Eggs and Ham" and was actually an "egg" made out of shaped honeydew and cantaloupe, and the ham was actually sliced prosciutto. The main course was a whole salmon steamed in the dishwasher. "You should have seen the look on everyone's faces when I took that fish out of the dishwasher instead of the oven." The dessert was "french fries" that were actually toasted pound cake strips placed in McDonald's french-fry boxes. "I passed ketchup bottles on the side that were filled with raspberry sauce," said Hanahan.

When asked what type of cuisine is the groups favorite to make, Hanahan says, "Each member is unique and has her own specialties. Ruth Bond is fabulous at Asian, Wilma Hall is a caterer and can do absolutely anything, and Bonnie Hale and I profess we don't cook at all except one time a year for this group, so our specialty is creativity."

Other cooking club events have included a gathering where they made their own sushi, a "guess the ingredient" theme, and a spectacular picnic basket luncheon. "We have even done a farewell to Martha Stewart event," says Proctor. "We wrote to her in jail when she was convicted, except we like to refer to her time away as *camp*, not jail."

For this group, having fun is second nature. "I would say our biggest budget is alcohol," Hanahan says with a laugh. "We definitely don't skimp on the drinks." While these women know how to have fun together, they do charity work together as well. Through the Bay Point Women's Club, they donate their time to Habitat for Humanity as well as local church organizations throughout Bay County. They have also donated a progressive dinner party for eight that was auctioned off at the club. "It feels good to give back," says Hanahan.

*From Mulligatawny to Pork Vindaloo,*
*The Table Is Set; All That's Missing Is You!*
*Please Join Me As We Celebrate the Colorful and*
*Exotic Flavors of India*

### Menu

Lychee Martinis

Indian-Spiced Fried Calamari with Tomato Chutney

Mulligatawny Soup

Pork Vindaloo with Raita Refresher

Coconut Rice

Roasted Curried Cauliflower, Potatoes, and Peas

Palak Paneer

Gulab Jamun (Fried Milk Balls in Cardamom Syrup)

# Lychee Martinis

*It's hard to describe the taste of lychees, except to say they have a distinctly fragrant and perfumey flavor. They grow abundantly in India and are common in Indian cuisine. These martinis are perfect for entertaining because they are so fast and easy to make. Make sure to really shake the cocktail shaker vigorously so that you'll get lots of tiny ice chips floating on the surface of your cocktails—they're the best part!*

Makes 8 martinis

> Two 15-ounce cans lychees in heavy syrup
> 2 cups vodka

Drain the lychees, reserving the syrup in 1 bowl and the fruit in another. You should have 2 cups of syrup. For each martini, skewer 1 or 2 lychees with a toothpick and place them in a chilled martini glass. Pour ¼ cup syrup and ¼ cup vodka into a martini shaker filled with ice. Shake the ingredients vigorously and strain into a martini glass. Repeat for the remaining cocktails.

# Indian-Spiced Fried Calamari with Tomato Chutney

*Dina loves fried calamari, and she didn't mind at all when, for a while, it seemed as if it was on every restaurant menu—except at Indian restaurants. So she came up with her own version to complement an Indian-themed dinner. The Tomato Chutney is also delicious served over grilled fish, chicken, or shrimp. For directions on cleaning squid,* *see page 104.*

Makes 8 servings

> 1 cup all-purpose flour
> 1 cup cornstarch
> 2 teaspoons paprika
> 1 teaspoon ground coriander
> 1 teaspoon ground cardamom
> 1 teaspoon ground cumin

4 pounds cleaned calamari, with tentacles, bodies cut into ½-inch rings
Salt
About 2 quarts vegetable oil for frying
Tomato Chutney (recipe follows)

Mix the flour, cornstarch, paprika, coriander, cardamom, and cumin in a shallow pan. Toss the calamari in the flour mixture to coat completely.

Fill a large, heavy pot with 3 inches of oil. Heat the oil over high heat until it reaches 350°F. Carefully, add the calamari to the oil in batches (the calamari may splatter a bit), and fry until the coating is brown and crispy, about 1 minute. Remove the calamari with a slotted spoon and drain it on paper towels. Season calamari with salt while still hot. Make sure that the oil temperature is at 350°F before adding each batch. Serve the hot calamari immediately with the Tomato Chutney for dipping.

## Tomato Chutney
Makes 1½ cups or enough for 8 servings

2 large tomatoes (about 1 pound), chopped
¼ cup finely diced red onion
2 tablespoons red wine vinegar
2 cloves garlic, minced
1 teaspoon minced fresh gingerroot
½ teaspoon salt
¼ teaspoon freshly ground black pepper
2 tablespoons chopped fresh mint leaves
2 tablespoons chopped fresh cilantro

In a medium-size saucepan over medium heat, combine the tomatoes, onion, vinegar, garlic, ginger, salt, and pepper. Bring them to a boil, then reduce the heat and simmer, uncovered, for 20 minutes. Remove the pan from the heat, stir in the mint and cilantro, and pour the chutney into a serving bowl. The chutney can be made a day in advance. Bring the chutney to room temperature before serving.

# Mulligatawny Soup

*Ever since we saw the* Seinfeld *"Soup Nazi" episode, in which Kramer's favorite soup is the mulligatawny, we have wanted to travel to New York to try it. Regrettably, the legendary Soup Kitchen closed in 2006 and we never got to taste the soup or hear the infamous Soup Nazi yell, "No soup for you!" Mulligatawny is a highly spiced Indian soup; in fact, "mulligatawny" literally means "pepper water." This version is not overly fiery, however, so don't be scared off by the name. If you'd like more heat, feel free to add extra jalapeños, along with their seeds (the hottest part). We often add some cooked shredded chicken to make the soup a complete meal. This soup is very filling, and the texture is thick and stewlike, so when serving for a cooking club gathering with several other courses, we recommend you limit the serving size to about a half cup. Note: You can find ghee, garam masala, turmeric, and curry leaves at Indian markets.*

Makes 8 to 10 full servings

¼ cup ghee (clarified butter) or vegetable oil

1 large onion, chopped

2 large carrots, cut into ¼-inch dice

2 stalks celery, cut into ¼-inch  dice

2 medium Granny Smith apples, peeled, cored, and cut into ¼-inch dice

2 jalapeños, stemmed, seeded, and minced

2 tablespoons minced garlic

2 tablespoons minced fresh ginger root

2 tablespoons garam masala

1 teaspoon ground turmeric

1 teaspoon ground cinnamon

½ teaspoon cayenne pepper

2 large potatoes, peeled and cut into ¼-inch  dice

1½ cups dried red lentils

15 fresh curry leaves, or 2 bay leaves

9 cups vegetable or chicken stock

2 teaspoons salt

One 13.5-ounce can unsweetened coconut milk

⅓ cup freshly squeezed lemon juice (about 1⅔ lemons)

Salt and freshly ground black pepper

2 cups cooked basmati rice

¼ cup chopped fresh cilantro

Heat the ghee in a large pot over medium-high heat. Add the onion, carrots, and celery and sauté, stirring often, until the vegetables are lightly browned, about 10 to 12 minutes. Add the apples, jalapeños, garlic, ginger, garam masala, turmeric, cinnamon, and cayenne, and sauté until the apples are caramelized, about 7 to 8 minutes. Add the potatoes, lentils, curry leaves, stock, and salt. Increase the heat to high and bring the soup to a boil. Reduce the heat, bringing the soup to a simmer, and cook, uncovered, until the lentils and all the vegetables are tender, about 25 to 30 minutes.

Whisk in the coconut milk and lemon juice and season with salt and pepper to taste. Simmer gently for 2 to 3 minutes to blend the flavors.

To serve the soup, spoon ¼ cup of rice into a warmed soup bowl, and pour 1 cup of soup over the rice. If you are making this dish for cooking club as part of an 8-course menu, only serve ⅛ cup of rice with ½ cup of soup. Garnish with the cilantro.

# Pork Vindaloo with Raita Refresher

*Vindaloo, a fiery sweet and sour dish, originated in the Portuguese-Indian colony of Goa. It is considered one of the spiciest Indian dishes, but it did not start out that way. The Goans named it after its two key ingredients:* vinho, *which means wine vinegar, and* alhos, *which means garlic. Vindaloo can be made with lamb, chicken, shrimp, or pork. The heat comes from the cayenne pepper, the sweetness from the cloves and cinnamon, and the sourness from the tamarind and vinegar. The combination makes for one of the most mouthwatering Indian dishes ever. If you favor the fiery, hot intensity this dish is known for, you can add more cayenne to your taste. The accompanying Raita Refresher, a cooling yogurt salad, will balance out the heat. Note: You can find black mustard seeds, garam masala, tamarind concentrate, ghee, and curry leaves at Indian markets.*

Makes 8 servings

> 1 teaspoon whole cloves
> 1 teaspoon black mustard seeds
> 2 teaspoons garam masala
> 1 teaspoon turmeric
> 1 teaspoon ground cinnamon
> ½ to 1 teaspoon cayenne pepper
> ⅓ cup white wine vinegar
> ⅓ cup tamarind concentrate or paste
> 8 cloves garlic
> 2 tablespoons roughly chopped fresh gingerroot
> 2 tablespoons ghee (clarified butter) or vegetable oil
> 3 pounds boneless pork shoulder, trimmed of fat and cut
>    into 1½-inch cubes
> 1½ teaspoons salt
> Freshly ground black pepper
> 1 large onion, thinly sliced
> 1 cup water
> One 14.5-ounce can diced tomatoes with their juices
> 15 fresh curry leaves, or 2 bay leaves
> 2 teaspoons sugar
> 1 red bell pepper, cut into 1-inch pieces
> Raita Refresher (recipe follows)

Heat a small skillet over medium-high heat. Add the whole cloves and black mustard seeds and dry roast them until they become fragrant, about 2 minutes. Put the cloves and mustard seeds into a blender jar and add the garam masala, turmeric, cinnamon, cayenne, vinegar, tamarind, garlic, and ginger. Blend at high speed until a smooth paste has formed. Set aside.

Heat the ghee in a large pot over medium-high heat. Season the pork with salt and pepper. In batches, brown the pork evenly on all sides, turning frequently with a slotted spoon, about 2 to 3 minutes per side. As the pieces brown, transfer them to a bowl.

Add the onions to the pot and sauté, stirring frequently, until the onions have lightly caramelized, about 10 or 12 minutes. Add the spice paste to the onions and sauté until fragrant, about 2 minutes. Add the water, tomatoes, curry leaves, sugar, and pork and bring to a boil over high heat. Reduce the heat to medium-low and simmer, covered, for 1½ hours, or until the pork is very tender when pierced with a fork. Add the red bell pepper and cook for 5 to 10 minutes more, or until the peppers are just crisp-tender. Serve hot with a dollop of the Raita Refresher and some Coconut Rice on the side.

## Raita Refresher

Makes 6 cups or enough for 8 servings

>  1 quart plain whole-milk yogurt
>  1 large unpeeled English hothouse cucumber, cut into ⅛-inch dice
>  2 tablespoons chopped fresh mint leaves
>  1 teaspoon salt
>  ¼ teaspoon freshly ground black pepper
>  1 tablespoon extra-virgin olive oil

Mix together the yogurt, cucumber, mint, salt, and pepper in a large bowl. Cover and chill until ready to serve. Just before serving, drizzle the oil over the raita. The raita can be made up to 1 day in advance.

# Coconut Rice

*This is the ideal rice dish to serve at a curry banquet. The coconut milk lends a subtle sweet-ness, and the simplicity and minimalism of the recipe perfectly complements the curries.*

Makes 8 servings

> 3 cups basmati rice
> Two 13.5-ounce cans unsweetened coconut milk
> 2 cups water
> 1 teaspoon salt
> ½ cup sliced toasted almonds, for garnish
> 3 tablespoons chopped fresh cilantro leaves, for garnish

Put the rice in a large, heavy saucepan. Stir in the coconut milk, water, and salt and bring to a boil over high heat. Reduce the heat, cover, and simmer for 20 minutes, or until the liquid is absorbed and the rice is tender. Fluff with a fork and serve warm on a large platter, garnished with the almonds and cilantro.

# Roasted Curried Cauliflower, Potatoes, and Peas

*When Dina eats Indian food, she often thinks that perhaps she could convert to vegetari-anism (although the thought vanishes the minute she smells a grilled lamb chop). Vegetar-ian dishes like this curry are her favorites. We love the caramelized flavors that roasting brings to the vegetables, which, combined with the delicious essence of the curry spices, puts this dish right over the top. Tiny black mustard seeds have no fragrance, but they are highly flavorful and are an essential ingredient in this recipe. You can find them at Indian markets and gourmet specialty stores.*

Makes 10 servings

> ¼ cup vegetable oil
> 1 tablespoon black mustard seeds
> 2 tablespoons curry powder, preferably Madras
> 1 tablespoon grated fresh gingerroot

1 tablespoon minced garlic

1 tablespoon sugar

2 teaspoons coarse salt

½ teaspoon freshly ground black pepper

1 large onion, peeled and quartered

2 heads cauliflower, cut into florets

2 pounds russet potatoes, peeled and cut into ½-inch pieces

1 cup frozen peas, thawed

2 tablespoons freshly squeezed lemon juice (about ⅔ lemon)

Salt and freshly ground black pepper

¼ cup chopped fresh cilantro

Preheat the oven to 475°F.

Whisk together the oil, mustard seeds, curry, ginger, garlic, sugar, salt, and pepper in a large bowl. Pull apart the onion quarters into separate layers. Toss the onion, cauliflower, and potatoes with the curry mixture.

Distribute the mixture equally on 2 large, rimmed baking sheets, and spread the vegetables in a single layer. Put 1 baking sheet in the middle of the oven and the other on the lower rack. Roast for 30 minutes, switching the baking sheets halfway through the roasting time. The cauliflower should be tender and browned in spots, and the potatoes should be just tender. Add the peas and roast for 5 more minutes. You can roast the vegetables up to 2 hours ahead, if desired. Rewarm them in a 450°F oven for 10 minutes.

Mound the vegetables in a large bowl. Season them with the lemon juice and with salt and pepper to taste, then sprinkle with the cilantro. Serve warm or at room temperature.

# Palak Paneer

*Palak paneer, also called saag paneer, is a spiced creamed spinach mixed with little cubes of fresh cheese called paneer. This may not be "pretty" food, but palak paneer is so delicious you will immediately forgive its lack of eye appeal. It is one of those dishes we return to over and over again. Serve it over the Coconut Rice on page 40 with some naan or flatbread brushed with ghee, and you have a feast. Note: You can find ghee and paneer at Indian markets.*

Makes 8 servings

2 pounds fresh spinach, washed, stems trimmed
1 cup water
1 cup packed fresh cilantro
2 tablespoons ghee
1 pound paneer, cut into ½-inch cubes
2 large onions, finely chopped
1 tablespoon minced garlic
1 tablespoon minced fresh gingerroot
2 teaspoons ground coriander
1½ teaspoons salt
1 teaspoon ground cumin
½ teaspoon ground cinnamon
½ teaspoon ground cloves
¼ teaspoon freshly ground black pepper
1 cup plain yogurt

Cook the spinach in the water in a large pot over high heat until wilted, about 7 minutes. Pour the spinach along with the water into a blender jar or a food processor fitted with a steel blade. Add the cilantro and purée until the mixture is smooth and velvety. Set aside.

Melt the ghee in a large skillet over medium-high heat. Add the paneer and fry, gently turning occasionally, until all sides are lightly browned, about 3 minutes. Transfer the paneer with a slotted spoon to a paper towel–lined dish to drain.

Add the onions to the skillet and sauté until lightly golden, about 15 minutes. Stir in the garlic, ginger, coriander, salt, cumin, cinnamon, cloves, and pepper, and cook for 1 minute. Add the puréed spinach. Lower the heat to medium and let the sauce simmer until thickened and almost all liquid is evaporated, about 2 to 4 minutes. Remove the pan from the heat, add the yogurt, and stir until blended. Gently fold in the paneer and serve warm.

# Gulab Jamun (Fried Milk Balls in Cardamom Syrup)

*Dina's friend Dolly Sood runs an Indian catering company called Good Karma Vegetarian Indian Food. One day she called and asked if Dina could help her cook for an event. Jumping at the chance to learn from Dolly, Dina arrived eager and ready, and by the time the party was over, they had served more than 100 people some of the best Indian food Dina has ever tasted. One of the most highly praised dishes that evening was Dolly's Gulab Jamun, and she was kind enough to share her recipe.*

Makes 24 balls or enough for 8 servings

> 1 cup full-fat milk powder
> ½ cup baking mix, such as Bisquick
> ½ cup heavy cream
> 2 cups water
> 2 cups sugar
> 2 green cardamom pods, crushed
> Canola oil for frying
> 2 tablespoons finely chopped raw pistachios

To prepare the milk balls, put the powdered milk, baking mix, and cream into a large bowl and stir until combined. Knead the dough until it feels oily in your hands, about 2 minutes. Portion the dough into 24 pieces, roll each piece into a ball with the palms of your hands, and set aside. Each ball will be about ½ inch in diameter. They will get bigger as they are fried and again after soaking in the syrup.

To make the syrup, in a large saucepan, bring the water, sugar, and cardamom to a boil over high heat. Once the syrup comes to a boil and the sugar has dissolved, remove it from the heat and set aside.

To fry the milk balls, heat the oil in a large, heavy pot to a moderate heat, about 230°F. Add the balls in batches of 4 or 5 at a time, and fry until they puff up a bit and turn golden brown, about 10 to 15 minutes. Stir them gently as they are frying to ensure that all sides are browned. Remove them with a slotted spoon and let them drain on a paper towel.

Once the fried milk balls have drained, add them to the warm syrup. Let them steep in the syrup for a minimum of 2½ hours and up to overnight.

To serve, gently remove the gulab jamun from the syrup with a slotted spoon and place three on each dish. Sprinkle with the chopped pistachios. Serve at room temperature.

*The discovery of a new dish does more for human happiness than the discovery of a new star.*

—Jean Anthelme Brillat-Savarin

## Tips for a Successful
# Indian-Inspired Dinner

- Shop at Indian stores for inexpensive fabrics to drape over the dining room chairs and to use as table runners. Color is a must, so don't be timid. Play with many different color combinations.

- Use gold costume jewelry bracelets for napkin rings at the place settings, and let guests take the bracelets home as a party gift.

- For instant ambience, burn incense in your bathroom. It will keep your whole house fragrant without being too overpowering.

- Throw a "Bollywood" party, with all the color and glamour of the Indian movie scene. Hang Indian movie posters on the walls, and have Bollywood soundtracks or movies playing in the background.

- Hire a henna artist to apply henna tattoos to your guests' hands or feet while you serve drinks and appetizers.

- Sprinkle cardamom pods decoratively along the table like confetti.

- Little carved elephants can be bought inexpensively at trade markets. Put one at each guest's place setting as a party favor.

# The U.N.K. Cooking Club

Kearney, Nebraska, is a small, tight-knit college town whose claim to fame might be the sandhill cranes that descend upon it once a year starting in March. This town of 28,000 residents swells with over 500,000 cranes, almost 90 percent of the world's entire sandhill crane population, which converge on the Platte River Valley to fuel up before they resume their northward migration. One of Kearney's other claims to fame is the U.N.K. Cooking Club (at least to the members who attend).

"Enjoying good food together is a common bond," says Diana Luscher. "Even if we don't attend the same church, have kids in the same schools, or share the same hobbies, food unites us all." Luscher is a longtime member of the cooking club, which was formed by female faculty members and female spouses at the University of Nebraska at Kearney. Their women-only club has been bonding through food since 2002.

"Our group just keeps growing," says Luscher. "We invite the new female faculty members and the female spouses to join us when they first arrive at the school. The only requirement is an interest in good food. Joining this group gives new members who enjoy cooking a way to get involved quickly with folks who have similar interests in food."

The hostess chooses the theme and cooks the main dish, and the other participants make the appetizers, side dishes, bread, and dessert, all in keeping with the chosen theme. They meet every other month and collectively choose the side dishes and appetizers to go with the stated theme. The hostess coordinates with each member a dish that would go well with the main course, and the guests decide what they would like to bring. Typically, each event will have eight or ten people attending.

"Eclectic" is the word Luscher uses to describe her cooking club. Many of the members are well traveled, and their love of travel inspires them in choosing the themes. "I choose themes based on places that I have traveled to and that I miss," says Luscher. "France, Portugal, Spain, and Mexico are just a few of the theme dinners that I have hosted." Some of the many cuisines explored by the club over the last seven years include Mexican, Spanish, Indian, Greek, Chinese, Caribbean, Italian, Filipino, and French.

"We all have bonded through our love of food and have become great friends," says Luscher. "Since we all have the University of Nebraska at Kearney as our connection, we socialize with each other in a lot of different settings such as sporting events, concerts, and other functions throughout the community."

When asked what her most memorable cooking club experience was, Luscher cheerily talks of a meeting that took place several years ago. "I hosted a Christmas dinner with all the trimmings and made a prime rib roast. The exhaust fan went out on my oven about halfway through the cooking time. Cooking the meat at such a high temperature, with the drippings spattering in the oven, we had a lot of smoke, and the fire alarm was set off more than once that night." The house was filled with billows of smoke that permeated all of the furniture, as well as the guests' coats on the coat rack in the living room, not to mention the guests themselves. She adds, "It took a few weeks for me to finally be rid of the smell of smoke. Everyone took the smoky evening in stride though and I am happy to say that the roast was cooked to absolute perfection."

In any small town, the people who live there are what make it great. Being able to live in a close community is a wonderful thing. "Bonding through food through the U.N.K. group has been such a gift," says Luscher.

And to us, that can only be described as "absolute perfection."

# Spring Has Sprung!
## A Garden Party on the Patio

*Winter Is Over; Get Ready for Spring!*
*Let's Meet on the Patio for an Outdoor Spring Fling*

### Menu

Tangerine Caipiroska

Spring Vegetable Bagna Cauda

Springtime Pea Salad with Pea Tendrils and Radishes
in a Tangy Lemon Dressing

Chilled Asparagus Soup with Lemon Cream

Easy Cheesy Biscuits

Halibut in Lettuce Packets with Fresh Lime and Dill Butter

Individual Creamy Potato-Leek Gratins Baked in Cream

Individual Frozen Tangerine Soufflés

# Tangerine Caipiroska

*This drink should be the official springtime refresher. It's pretty, it's light, and it's a perfect way to celebrate the arrival of warm weather. A variation on the Brazilian Caipirinha, it uses vodka instead of the traditional cachaça. You can increase the recipe according to the number of people you are serving, muddling the fruit in the bottom of a serving pitcher, but we think these drinks are best made individually. Note: Be careful not to muddle the limes too much, as this can make them bitter and ruin an otherwise perfect cocktail.*

Makes 1 cocktail

> ½ small, sweet tangerine, peeled, extra pith removed
> ¼ lime plus more for garnish
> 2 teaspoons superfine sugar
> 2 ounces good-quality vodka
> Crushed ice

Put the tangerine, lime, and sugar in a rocks glass or small tumbler and muddle them with the back of a wooden spoon. Add enough ice to come to the top of the glass, then add the vodka. Give it a quick stir and serve, garnished with a lime wedge.

# Spring Vegetable Bagna Cauda

*A bagna cauda is a warm oil dipping sauce, somewhat like an oil fondue. Choose fresh, perfect seasonal vegetables straight from your garden or farmers market. Some of our favorites for a bagna cauda are fennel bulbs, tiny artichokes, baby turnips, asparagus spears, young fava beans, small carrots, Belgian endive, cauliflower, radicchio, and multicolored radishes.*

Makes 8 servings

> 1 cup extra-virgin olive oil
> 4 tablespoons unsalted butter
> 6 oil-packed anchovy fillets
> 1 teaspoon freshly grated lemon zest
> 6 cloves garlic
> ¼ teaspoon freshly ground black pepper
> One 1-pound crusty country loaf, cut into 1-inch cubes
> Assorted fresh spring vegetables, cut into bite-size pieces (enough to make
>     4 cups)

Put the oil, butter, anchovies, lemon zest, garlic, and pepper in the bowl of a food processor fitted with a steel blade and pulse until smooth. Transfer the mixture to a medium-size saucepan and cook over low heat for 10 to 15 minutes, stirring occasionally until flavors are incorporated and mixture is bubbly. Do not be concerned if the sauce separates. Pour the hot sauce into a fondue pot and set the pot over its heat source to keep warm. Serve with vegetables and bread for dipping.

# Springtime Pea Salad with Pea Tendrils and Radishes in a Tangy Lemon Dressing

*To get the most of the flavors of spring, we recommend using fresh shelled peas rather than frozen. The latter will work, but the sweetness of the fresh peas really makes this salad. If you are not going to serve the salad immediately, you can make the dressing up to a day in advance and store it in the refrigerator until you are ready to serve. However, do not mix the sliced radish with the peas until the last minute, or they will lose their crunch.*

Makes 8 servings

4 cups shelled fresh peas (about 4 pounds), or two 10-ounce packages of frozen baby peas

½ cup thinly sliced radishes (about 3 large radishes)

1 cup loosely packed pea tendrils, cut into 3-inch lengths

¼ cup extra-virgin olive oil

3 tablespoons freshly squeezed lemon juice (about 1 lemon)

1 tablespoon finely minced fresh tarragon

2 shallots, finely minced

Salt and freshly ground black pepper

2 heads butter lettuce, washed and drained

To prepare the vegetables, put the peas in a large pot of boiling salted water over medium-high heat. Cook the peas until almost tender, about 5 minutes. Immediately remove them from the heat, rinse under very cold water to stop the cooking process, and drain. Add the radishes and the pea tendrils to the peas and stir. Set aside.

To make the dressing, combine the olive oil, lemon juice, tarragon, and shallots and mix well. Season with salt and pepper to taste. Drizzle the dressing over the pea mixture and mix gently until just combined.

To serve the salad, separate the leaves from the heads of lettuce and choose 8 of the largest leaves. Place a lettuce leaf on each plate. Spoon about ½ cup of the pea mixture on top of each lettuce leaf.

*We should look for someone to eat and drink with before looking for*
*something to eat and drink . . .*
—Epicurus

*Tips for a Successful*
## Springtime Dinner

- For your party invitations, use springtime pastel colors—pale pink, lavender, green, or yellow. Attach a sprig of dried lavender or other dried spring flower.

- Fill small watering containers with moss. Add plastic bugs, tiny bird's eggs, and gardening tools, or other symbols of spring. Use them as a centerpiece, or place them decoratively on a side table. String handmade crepe flowers together with fine string or fishing line and hang them from an outside patio structure, tree branches, or a trellis.

- Place tiny lights in the trees that surround your outdoor dining table, or on the fence or garage. This creates a magical effect in the evening.

- Use herb seed packets in miniature terra-cotta pots or a potted blooming tulip or daffodil bulb for party favors.

- Make a table runner of green "cat grass" down the center of your table. Place tea lights or floating candles decoratively throughout. Trays of cat grass can be purchased inexpensively at pet stores, and when grouped together, they make a stunning table presentation.

# Chilled Asparagus Soup with Lemon Cream

*Asparagus, one of our favorite vegetables, is a delicious harbinger of spring. This soup, which is a beautiful, vibrant green, can be served either hot or cold.*

Makes 8 servings

½ cup sour cream
3 tablespoons freshly squeezed lemon juice (about 1 lemon)
½ teaspoon freshly grated lemon zest

2 pounds fresh asparagus, ends trimmed
4 tablespoons unsalted butter
2 small leeks, white and tender green parts only, halved,
    cut into ½-inch slices
4 cloves garlic, chopped
6 cups chicken stock
2 cups fresh spinach leaves, chopped
1 cup fresh flat-leaf parsley, chopped
1 teaspoon salt
¼ teaspoon freshly ground black pepper
Pinch cayenne pepper

To make the lemon cream, mix together the sour cream, lemon juice, and zest in a small bowl, and set it aside in the refrigerator until ready to serve.

To prepare the soup, coarsely chop the asparagus spears. Set aside the asparagus tips until ready to serve. Melt the butter in a large, heavy saucepan over medium heat. Add the leeks and garlic and sauté for about 5 minutes, until soft but not browned. Add the asparagus and stock and bring to a boil over high heat; boil for 2 minutes. Reduce the heat to medium, add the spinach and parsley, and simmer for 5 minutes. Add the salt, pepper, and cayenne and remove the pan from the heat. Let the soup cool to room temperature.

Working in batches, purée the soup in a blender or food processor until smooth, then pour it through a strainer into a storage container. Taste the soup and adjust the seasoning if necessary. Put the soup in the refrigerator to cool for at least 2 hours, or up to a day in advance before serving.

Serve the soup chilled, garnishing each portion with the lemon cream and reserved raw asparagus tips.

# Easy Cheesy Biscuits

*When Michelle was working as a pastry chef, it probably would have hurt her brain a little bit to use a prepackaged baking mix, but now that she's a mom living in suburbia, it doesn't bother her one little bit! And to get that authentic flavor of the biscuits served at Red Lobster restaurants, the mix is a must. These biscuits are perfect with almost any fish dish, and they are so easy to make. They will be gobbled up quickly, so consider doubling the recipe.*

Makes 12 biscuits

> ½ stick (4 tablespoons) unsalted butter, melted
> ½ teaspoon garlic powder
> ¼ teaspoon seafood seasoning, such as Old Bay
> 2 cups biscuit mix, such as Bisquick
> ½ cup grated Parmesan cheese
> 1 cup grated sharp cheddar cheese
> 1 teaspoon dried onion flakes
> ⅔ cup milk

Preheat the oven to 450°F.

Combine the melted butter, garlic powder, and seafood seasoning in a small bowl. Set aside.

In a large bowl, combine the biscuit mix, Parmesan, cheddar, dried onion flakes, and milk, stirring well. Drop the batter by rounded teaspoonfuls about 2 inches apart onto an ungreased cookie sheet. After 4 or 5 minutes, remove the biscuits from the oven and brush the tops evenly with the melted butter mixture. Continue baking for 4 to 5 minutes more, or until golden brown. Serve warm.

# Halibut in Lettuce Packets with Fresh Lime and Dill Butter

*Michelle's parents Sherry and Dennis live part-time in Alaska and love fishing for halibut. This recipe is inspired by a dish her mom likes to make. This is a real show-off dish, and it makes for a fun and beautiful presentation at the table. The fish packages can be assembled a few hours ahead and then put in the oven at the last minute, making this the perfect dish for entertaining. Note: Buy the largest head of butter lettuce you can find. Depending on the size of the butter lettuces at your market, you may need to buy an extra head so you'll have enough of the largest leaves for making the packets.*

Makes 8 servings

½ pound (2 sticks) unsalted butter, softened
2 tablespoons freshly squeezed lime juice (about 1 lime)
2 tablespoons chopped fresh dill
2 tablespoons chopped fresh chives
5 teaspoons freshly grated lime zest
½ teaspoon salt
¼ teaspoon freshly ground black pepper

Eight large butter lettuce leaves
Eight 1-inch-thick halibut fillets, about 4 ounces each
1 medium-size red bell pepper, cut into thin strips
1 medium-size yellow bell pepper, cut into thin strips
8 ⅛-inch-thick lime slices

Preheat the oven to 450°F.

To make the dill butter, combine the butter, lime juice, dill, chives, lime zest, salt, and pepper in a small bowl and mix until blended. Set aside.

To prepare the lettuce packets, cut eight 10-inch squares of both parchment paper and aluminum foil. Remove the inner stalk of each lettuce leaf, dividing each leaf into halves. This makes it easier to roll the lettuce evenly. For each of the 8 packets, place 2 half leaves side by side, slightly overlapping, on a square of parchment paper.

To assemble, arrange the fish fillets on top of the leaves. Spread the fillets with equal amounts of the dill butter; arrange some red and yellow pepper strips over the fillets, and top each fillet with a lime slice. Fold up the lower edge of the leaves to cover the fillet, leaving the sides open. Enclose each lettuce packet tightly in the parchment and then the aluminum foil.

To cook and serve the fish, arrange the packets on a shallow baking sheet. Bake the packets until the fish is opaque in the center, about 15 minutes (unwrap the foil and parchment from one of the fish packets to test for doneness). Remove only the foil layer and serve the packets still inside the parchment for your guests to unwrap at the table.

# Individual Creamy Potato-Leek Gratins Baked in Cream

*The simplicity of this dish wows us every time. This is hands-down our favorite way to serve potatoes for company, and even Michelle's kids, who don't like potatoes, wolf these down. This dish is perfect for company because you can prepare the potato mixture ahead of time, then bake off the gratins just before serving. Low calorie this is not, so save this dish for a special occasion when you want to impress. Note: For this recipe, you will need eight individual 6-ounce ovenproof gratin dishes.*

Makes 8 servings

> 5 medium-size Idaho potatoes
> 2 tablespoons unsalted butter
> 2 leeks, white and tender green parts only, washed thoroughly, and cut into thin slices (about 2 cups)
> 3½ cups heavy cream
> 2 tablespoons chopped fresh parsley
> ¼ teaspoon grated nutmeg
> 1 teaspoon salt
> ¼ teaspoon freshly ground black pepper

Preheat the oven to 375°F.

Peel the potatoes and cut them into very thin slices (about ⅛-inch thick). Melt the butter in a heavy-bottomed saucepan over medium heat until it just starts to foam. Add the leeks and cook until translucent, about 3 to 5 minutes. Slowly add the cream and bring to a boil; add the parsley, nutmeg to taste, salt, and pepper.

Fold the potatoes into the cream, making sure each potato is coated well. Simmer the potatoes over medium heat until the cream starts to thicken and the potatoes are almost tender, about 10 minutes. If you are serving the gratins at a later date, put the mixture in a tightly covered container and refrigerate until you are ready to proceed. The potatoes can be prepared up to this point up to 2 days ahead.

Spoon a layer of the potato and cream mixture about 1½ inches deep into 8 gratin dishes. Bake the gratins for 25 to 30 minutes, or until the potatoes are golden brown and tender enough that a knife can slide easily into them. Serve hot.

# Individual Frozen Tangerine Soufflés

*When Michelle was enrolled in the pastry course at Tante Marie's Cooking School in San Francisco, frozen soufflés were one of her favorite desserts to make. She was amazed that something so beautiful, and that looked so difficult to make, could be so easy to prepare. Cold soufflés are made from a flavored mousse that has gelatin added to it, so unlike regular soufflés, they aren't baked in the oven to achieve that dramatic sky-high effect. This is a very nice thing indeed on a hot day when you don't want to use the oven. Over the years Michelle has made countless frozen soufflés, and this is one of her favorite flavors. This dessert is elegant and light, and the perfect ending to a spring meal. You can make the soufflés up to a day in advance and keep them in the freezer. Just be sure to remove them from the freezer an hour before serving. Note: For this recipe, you will need eight individual 1-cup soufflé dishes or ramekins; aluminum foil; and some kitchen string, rubber bands, or straight pins.*

Makes 8 servings

> 8 tangerines
> One ¼-ounce package (1 tablespoon) plain, unflavored gelatin
> ½ teaspoon pure vanilla extract

5 eggs, separated

¾ cups sugar

3 cups heavy cream

½ cup finely chopped raw pistachios

8 sprigs fresh mint for garnish, if desired

8 candied violets for garnish, if desired

To prepare the soufflé dishes or ramekins, cut a sheet of aluminum foil long enough to wrap around one of the dishes, and fold it lengthwise in quarters to make a band about 3 inches wide. Wrap the foil around the top of the dish, making a collar. The collar should extend about 2 inches above the rim of the soufflé dish. Overlap the ends of the foil and tape them together. Secure the collar in place with a rubber band or a straight pin, or tie it with kitchen string. Repeat for all 8 dishes.

To prepare the soufflé mixture, zest the 8 tangerines. You should have about 1½ tablespoons of zest. Juice 4 of the tangerines until you have ½ cup of juice, and strain out any pits. Reserve the other tangerines for another use. Put the juice and zest into a small saucepan set over low heat. When it just starts to come to a boil, sprinkle the gelatin over the tangerine juice and whisk until the gelatin dissolves completely. Add the vanilla extract and remove from the heat. Set aside.

Heat the egg yolks and sugar in a large metal bowl set over a pot of simmering water, making sure that the bowl does not come in contact with the water. Whisk constantly until the mixture is pale yellow and creamy, about 10 minutes. Remove the egg yolk mixture from the heat and allow it to cool.

In the bowl of a standing mixer fitted with the whisk attachment, beat the egg whites until they form stiff peaks, then set aside. In a separate large bowl, beat the cream until it forms soft peaks.

Spoon about half of the egg whites into the cooled egg yolk mixture, and gently stir to combine. Gently fold in the remaining egg whites to the lightened egg yolks. Next, gently fold the egg mixture into the whipped cream. Pour the tangerine mixture on top. Note: If the tangerine mixture has become too firm, set the pan back on the stove over low heat just long enough for it to become smooth again, then allow it to cool slightly. Gently fold the tangerine mixture and the egg–whipped cream mixture together until just combined, being careful not to over mix.

To assemble the soufflés, spoon the soufflé mixture into the prepared dishes or ramekins until it comes about halfway up the foil collar. Smooth the top and place the soufflés in the freezer until firm, about 4 hours. If you are making the soufflés in advance, once the mixture is firm, cover them with plastic wrap, making sure that the plastic adheres directly to the top of the soufflés, and freeze until ready to serve.

To serve, remove the soufflés from the freezer an hour before serving. Sprinkle the chopped pistachios over the tops, and carefully remove the foil collars. Garnish each soufflé with a mint sprig and a candied violet, if desired.

# The Town and Gown Gourmet Group

Candy Grover of Bloomington, Indiana, was originally a member of a very large cooking club at Indiana University, where her interest in cooking flourished. But she and others felt that the opportunity to really develop their cooking skills was inhibited in such a large group. They decided to split off and start their own smaller cooking club, and the Town and Gown Gourmet Group was formed in 1998.

Grover's cooking club has been going strong ever since. The group is made up of twelve couples, ages 26 to 70. "We are pretty diverse, but that's what keeps this group interesting. We all come from different backgrounds and age groups, but we are like minded, and that's what makes our group work," says Grover.

Grover's club is larger than many of the cooking clubs we have met. Most cooking clubs have home-size restrictions and find that there is too much food being served with large groups. The Town and Gown Gourmet Group has come up with a method that allows everyone an opportunity to attend a cooking club gathering in each person's home without things getting too crowded.

Each September, the club holds a cocktail party, which all twelve couples attend, usually in someone's backyard or a park. At this party, each couple receives the schedule for the year, assigned by Grover.

The twelve couples are split into three groups per hosting cycle, with four couples per group. While all twelve couples meet during each hosting cycle, they meet in different groups of four couples each time. Among the four couples per group, one couple is assigned hosting responsibilities, one couple is assigned co-hosting responsibilities, and the other two couples per group are assigned guest responsibilities. The hosting periods are October–November, January–February, March–April, and May–June, so the host couple has a two-month slot to choose a date that works for all four couples.

Grover rotates the groups to ensure that everyone has a chance to enjoy a cooking club gathering with all the club members at some point during the year. So, for example, if a couple hosts during the October–November hosting cycle, they would then co-host during another hosting period with three completely different couples, and become a guest couple during the remaining two hosting cycles, again with different couples.

The host is responsible for selecting the menu, making sure everyone attending the dinner receives the full menu and a copy of all of the recipes preferably at least two weeks before the dinner, selecting and providing the beverages, preparing their home, cleaning up after everyone leaves, and sometimes making one small dish. The co-host is assigned the entrée, and the guest couples are responsible for the side dishes, salads, appetizers, and dessert.

Invitations are typically sent via e-mail. If a recipe comes from a cookbook or a magazine, the host will usually type it up and send it with the invitation. "We're all pretty good typists in this group, so it's not a big deal for us to retype recipes and get them out that way," says Grover.

The Town and Gown Gourmet Group likes to use recipes from *Gourmet*, *Bon Appétit*, *Food and Wine*, and *Saveur* magazines, according to Grover. "Lately, though, we've been making a lot of dishes from *Arabesque: A Taste of Morocco, Turkey, and Lebanon*, by Claudia Roden and *Frank Stitt's Southern Table: Recipes and Gracious Traditions from Highlands Bar and Grill*," says Grover. "We love those two cookbooks."

When asked what she would recommend to someone trying to start a cooking club, Grover replies, "Recruit carefully. If you like to cook, you probably know a number of people who are like-minded, and they probably have friends you are not acquainted with who might be good members. We are all Slow Food members [an organization devoted to preserving traditional food ways and combating fast food], so joining an organization like that also gives you the opportunity to meet many like-minded people."

Recently, one of the couples from Grover's cooking club moved away, and they were looking for another couple to fill the vacancy. "One of our newest members in the past year is someone I met on Chowhound.com. She was looking for suggestions for Vietnamese food in Indianapolis. I answered, and it turns out that she lives within walking distance of my home, but we had never met."

Another recommendation Grover passed on is to have club guidelines. The guidelines in Grover's group spell out the host's and co-host's responsibilities, along with some scheduling and menu guidelines. "We have protocol suggestions—like the host should include, as part of the invitation, where others might be able to find unique ingredients, and offers to lend or find out-of-the-ordinary utensils, like a Pullman loaf pan," says Grover.

Finally, Grover recommends having a group leader. "Whether it is the same person every year, or it revolves among the members, it is a good idea to have someone take over the organizational duties. Without a leader or coordinator, it can be chaotic," says Grover.

As we ended our conversation, Grover was going to rush off and figure out how to make a risotto Milanese in her new pressure cooker. "The thing kind of scares me," says Grover. It's hard to believe a pressure cooker scares Grover considering she has skillfully coordinated 12 couples in a cooking club for over ten years. Brava!

# Smashing Plates:
## Greece Is the Word

*Opa!*

*Please Join Us for a Raucous Plate-Smashing, Toga-Wearing,*

*Big Fat Greek Dinner Party*

*Good Food and Good Times Are Sure to Be Had by All!*

### Menu

Melon, Mint, and Ouzo Cocktails

Feta-Stuffed Figs with Honey-Butter Glaze

Avgolemono Soup (Greek Chicken Soup with Egg and Lemon Sauce)

Arugula and Romaine Salad with Grilled Halloumi Cheese

Garlic-Crusted Rack of Lamb with Kalamata Olives
and Sun-Dried Tomatoes

Roasted Fingerling Potatoes with Lemon, Garlic, and Oregano

Imam Bayildi

Orange Galaktoboureko (Custard-Filled Phyllo Pastry)

# Melon, Mint, and Ouzo Cocktails

*The Greeks make a delicious dessert called* peponi me ouzo, *melon with ouzo. The canta-loupe is macerated for hours in ouzo (a Greek liqueur flavored with anise) and sugar before serving. Fruity cocktails are just dessert before dinner for us, so we created this drink to get our dessert in first. If anise is not your thing, use a Greek wine instead. Opa!*

Makes 8 servings

1 cup sugar
½ cup water
10 large fresh mint leaves

---

1 ripe 3-pound cantaloupe, peeled, seeded, and roughly chopped
½ cup mint syrup (recipe follows)
½ cup ouzo
2 cups vodka
3 tablespoons freshly squeezed lime juice (about 1 ½ limes)
1 cup ice cubes
8 sprigs fresh mint

To make the mint syrup, put the sugar, water, and mint leaves in a small sauce-pan over medium-high heat and, stirring occasionally, bring the mixture to a boil. Reduce the heat and simmer the syrup for 10 minutes. Remove the pan from the heat, cover, and let the syrup infuse for 20 minutes. Strain the mixture and chill thoroughly. The extra syrup will keep in the refrigerator for up to 5 days.

When you are ready to serve, purée the cantaloupe with ½ cup of the syrup in a blender until smooth. Add the ouzo, vodka, lime juice, and ice cubes to the blender. Process on high speed until the ice is crushed and the liquid is frothy. Garnish with the mint sprigs and serve in tall 8-ounce glasses.

# Feta-Stuffed Figs with Honey-Butter Glaze

*Dina grew up in a Middle Eastern household where mezes (assorted small appetizer-like dishes) were a major part of her cuisine, just as they are in Greek homes. Her mother often put olives, hummus, pita bread, yogurt, cheese, feta, eggplant dip, and more on the table for many of the meals. On very hot days, mezes make a perfect light meal. One favorite dish is* basturma *(also spelled* pastourma*), beef cured in a garlic-spice paste. Here, feta-stuffed figs are wrapped in basturma, baked, and drizzled with a honey-butter glaze. You can find basturma in Greek, Turkish, Armenian, and Middle Eastern stores. If you can't find it, you can substitute prosciutto.*

Makes 8 servings

16 large dried Greek figs, preferably Kalamatas
Boiling water
3 ounces crumbled feta cheese (about ¾ cup), at room temperature
2 tablespoons finely chopped walnuts
1 teaspoon finely chopped fresh oregano
16 thin slices *basturma* or prosciutto (about 4 ounces)
16 toothpicks

---

2 tablespoons unsalted butter
1 tablespoon honey
1 teaspoon lemon zest

---

2 tablespoons extra-virgin olive oil

Preheat the oven to 450°F.

Place the figs in a large, heatproof bowl. Cover them with boiling water and soak until plump, about 15 to 30 minutes. Drain the figs and set aside.

To make the stuffing, combine the feta, walnuts, and oregano in a small bowl. Cut the stem from the top of each fig. Make a vertical slit down the center of each fig, being careful not to cut through the base of the fig. Stuff each fig with about 1 teaspoon of the feta mixture, then gently press it closed to seal. Wrap each fig with a slice of basturma and secure it with a toothpick.

Note: You can prepare the figs a day ahead up to this point. Store the figs in the refrigerator in an airtight container. Let them stand at room temperature for an hour before baking.

To make the glaze, combine the butter, honey, and lemon zest in a small saucepan. Cook over medium heat for 10 minutes, until the butter melts. Stir the mixture to blend.

To finish, place the figs on a baking sheet and drizzle them with the oil. Bake until the basturma has browned, about 10 minutes, turning after 5 minutes to brown both sides evenly. Transfer the figs to a large platter. Drizzle the figs with the honey-butter glaze and serve warm.

# Avgolemono Soup (Greek Chicken Soup with Egg and Lemon Sauce)

*Avgolemono, an egg and lemon sauce, is probably one of the most well-known Greek sauces. It is used in many of their dishes from roasted meats to casseroles to stewed and stuffed vegetables. Our cooking club tried an avgolemono sauce over rice, and we all agreed it was delicious and would go in our repertoire of dishes. Avgolemono soup is our favorite way to use the sauce. It has a very creamy, light, and refreshing flavor to it—the perfect soup for a spring day.*

Makes 8 to 10 servings

>    1 whole roasting chicken, about 3 to 3½ pounds
>    12 cups cold water
>    1 large onion, quartered
>    2 large carrots, peeled, each cut into 3 or 4 pieces
>    2 celery stalks, each cut into 3 or 4 pieces
>    1 teaspoon whole black peppercorns
>    2 bay leaves
>    2 teaspoons salt
>    1 cup orzo
>    3 eggs

½ cup freshly squeezed lemon juice (about 2⅔ lemons)
2 tablespoons freshly chopped parsley for garnish

Put the chicken in a large stockpot. Add water to cover and bring nearly to a boil over moderate heat. Do not allow the water to boil or the stock will become cloudy. Reduce the heat to a gentle simmer and skim any foam from the surface with a slotted spoon. Once the liquid is clear, add the onion, carrots, celery, peppercorns, and bay leaves. Allow to simmer until the chicken is thoroughly cooked, about 1 hour.

Remove the chicken from the broth. Strain the broth into a large bowl and set aside. Discard the vegetables. Once the chicken is cool enough to handle, remove the skin and as much fat as possible and discard. Shred the remaining chicken meat with your fingers. Put the chicken in a large bowl and set aside. The broth and chicken can be refrigerated at this point and finished the next day. Chilling the broth makes it easier to skim the fat from the surface.

Shortly before serving, heat the broth in a large pot over high heat. Add the salt and orzo and bring to a boil. Reduce the heat to a simmer and cook, uncovered, until the orzo is cooked through, about 20 minutes.

Blend the eggs and lemon juice in a blender or food processor until well mixed. With the motor running, slowly add 2 cups of strained broth to the egg mixture. The sauce can be made by hand, using a whisk, as well; just be sure to whisk vigorously while adding the hot liquid to the egg mixture to keep the eggs from curdling.

Pour the egg-lemon sauce slowly into the remaining broth, whisking briskly. Add the reserved shredded chicken, heat gently for 1 or 2 minutes more, and serve, garnishing each bowl with a sprinkle of parsley.

*Dining with one's friends and beloved family is certainly
one of life's primal and most innocent delights, one that is both
soul-satisfying and eternal.*
—Julia Child

## Tips for a Successful
# Greek-Inspired Feast

- Use blue and white, the colors of the Greek flag, for your centerpiece, with blue and white fabrics for a table runner. Or set a pristine, white table accented with touches of blue.

- Send rolled-up invitations that look like Greek scrolls to your guests.

- Use a Greek myths theme, and ask guests to wear the costume of a different Greek god or goddess.

- Columns can be rented from party supply stores. Purchase ivy from floral supply stores, wrap ivy around columns, and arrange them around your home.

- When people think of Greek foods, they think of lemons, olives, eggplants, figs, parsley, and honey. Incorporate these foods into a stunning centerpiece.

- If you will be dining outside, hang an abundance of grape leaves and clusters of grapes overhead, suggesting a vineyard.

- Greece is known for its fabulous beaches. Evoke a sense of the beach with shells placed decoratively along the table.

- For the place settings, take large, white, clean shells and paint the name of each guest on them with a gold marker.

- Preserved lemons or cured olives packaged in a beautiful container make great gifts for your guests to take home.

- Have the soundtrack to *Zorba the Greek* playing when guests arrive.

# Arugula and Romaine Salad with Grilled Halloumi Cheese

*Halloumi is a fresh white cheese that tastes like a salted mozzarella. It has a high melting point, so it can be fried or grilled, which makes it turn wonderfully gooey and soft in the center with a delicious, crisp exterior. Halloumi cheese is from Cyprus, and you can usually find it at Greek, Turkish, Armenian, and Middle Eastern stores, or at cheese shops. We've also found it at Whole Foods Market.*

Makes 8 servings

½ cup extra-virgin olive oil
⅓ cup freshly squeezed lemon juice (about 1 ⅔ lemons)
2 cloves garlic, minced
1 tablespoon chopped fresh oregano
1 teaspoon coarse salt
¼ teaspoon freshly ground black pepper
1 large head (about 1 pound) romaine lettuce, trimmed, leaves coarsely
 torn into bite-size pieces
6 cups (about 5 ounces) arugula, leaves coarsely torn
8.5 ounces *halloumi* cheese, cut into 16 slices, each ¼-inch thick
Fresh oregano sprigs for garnish
2 lemons cut into 8 wedges for garnish

Whisk together the oil, lemon juice, garlic, oregano, salt, and pepper in a small bowl. Just before serving, toss the romaine lettuce and arugula with the dressing in a large bowl and set aside.

Heat a large nonstick skillet or grill pan over medium heat. Add the cheese slices and fry until golden, about 1 minute per side.

To serve, arrange the salad on a large platter and top it with the fried cheese. Remove the leaves from the oregano sprig and garnish the salad with oregano leaves and lemon wedges.

# Garlic-Crusted Rack of Lamb with Kalamata Olives and Sun-Dried Tomatoes

*Fellow cooking club member Carolyn Soriano is very good about wanting to take on dishes that she would typically avoid in order to test herself during our gatherings and expand her repertoire. Lamb is one of her specialties, and while it can be tricky to prepare well, this recipe is practically foolproof. The crust for the rack of lamb is also fantastic as a stuffing for a butterflied leg of lamb, if you prefer to use that cut of meat.*

Makes 8 servings

1 cup pitted kalamata olives
1 cup fresh bread crumbs from crusty baguette
½ cup oil-packed sun-dried tomatoes, drained well
4 teaspoons minced garlic
1 tablespoon chopped fresh oregano
Salt and freshly ground black pepper
2 tablespoons extra-virgin olive oil
Two 2-pound racks of lamb (8 chops each), trimmed and frenched
1½ teaspoons salt
½ teaspoon freshly ground pepper

Preheat the oven to 450°F.

Combine the olives, bread crumbs, sun-dried tomatoes, garlic, and oregano in the bowl of a food processor fitted with a steel blade and pulse until finely chopped. Season with salt and pepper to taste.

Heat the oil in a large, heavy skillet over medium-high heat. Season the lamb with the salt and pepper. When the oil is almost smoking, add 1 rack to the skillet, round side down. Brown it well, about 5 or 6 minutes. Put it in a roasting pan, round side up, and repeat with the remaining rack of lamb.

Let the lamb cool slightly. Using a spoon or your hands, spread the olive and bread crumb mixture evenly over the top of the lamb. Roast the lamb for 15 to 20 minutes for medium-rare, or until a thermometer inserted into the center registers 134°F. Let the lamb rest for 5 to 10 minutes before carving. Carve the rack into individual chops and serve.

# Roasted Fingerling Potatoes with Lemon, Garlic, and Oregano

*These mouth-watering Greek-style roasted potatoes are usually served alongside a roasted leg of lamb or a whole roasted chicken. In the old days, when most people's kitchens did not have ovens, Greek villagers would prepare their Sunday lamb roast and potatoes in a large pan and carry it to the local bakery first thing in the morning to bake in the communal oven. By lunchtime, their meal was cooked and ready to be picked up and enjoyed by the whole family. Even though ovens are now commonplace, some small village bakeries still offer that traditional service on Sundays. This recipe uses fingerling potatoes—small, thin potatoes with a smooth texture and a buttery flavor. You can usually find them at farmers markets or specialty food stores, and sometimes at supermarkets. Small new potatoes or red-skinned potatoes would work in their place.*

Makes 8 servings

3 dozen fingerling potatoes, about 3 pounds, cut in half lengthwise
½ cup extra-virgin olive oil
1 tablespoon minced garlic
1 tablespoon chopped fresh oregano, plus 1 teaspoon for garnish
1½ teaspoons coarse salt
½ teaspoon freshly ground black pepper
½ cup fat-free, low-sodium chicken stock
½ cup freshly squeezed lemon juice (about 2⅔ lemons)

Preheat the oven to 375°F.

In a large bowl, toss the potatoes with the oil, garlic, 1 tablespoon of the chopped oregano, salt, and pepper. Arrange them on a large rimmed baking sheet, cut side down, and roast for 20 minutes. Pour the chicken stock over the potatoes and roast for another 20 minutes. Pour the lemon juice over the potatoes and roast for a final 15 minutes, until the potatoes are tender on the inside and crisp on the outside.

Sprinkle the potatoes with the remaining oregano and serve.

# Imam Bayildi

*Although this eggplant dish has a Turkish name and may have originated in Turkey, it is a favorite in Greece as well. Imam bayildi is Turkish for "the priest fainted." Legend has it that a Turkish priest, or imam, was served this dish created by his wife, and upon consuming it, he fainted. There are several reasons given as to why. One is that he found it so delicious, he fainted in ecstasy. Another is that he fainted when he learned how much costly olive oil was used in the dish. Whatever the reason, with a great story like that, we had to try it for ourselves. (For the record, we're going with the "fainting because it was so good" version.) Have some smelling salts handy in case your guests faint with pleasure.*

Makes 8 servings

> 1 large globe eggplant (about 20 ounces), trimmed, cut into 8 rounds, each ½-inch thick
> 2 tablespoons coarse salt
> ½ cup plus 2 tablespoons extra-virgin olive oil
> 1 large red onion, chopped
> 2 tablespoons minced garlic
> 4 large (2 pounds) fresh tomatoes, chopped
> 2 tablespoons sugar
> ½ cup chopped fresh flat-leaf parsley
> 1 teaspoon dried thyme
> 1 teaspoon dried Greek oregano (use dried marjoram if Greek oregano is unavailable)
> 1½ teaspoons salt
> ½ teaspoon freshly ground black pepper
> 2 lemons, each cut into 4 wedges

Toss the eggplant with the salt in a large bowl, making sure the salt is evenly distributed on both sides of each eggplant slice. Put the eggplant in a colander set over a large bowl or baking sheet and set it aside for an hour. Rinse the eggplant and dry it thoroughly with paper towels.

Preheat the oven to 375°F.

Heat ¼ cup of the oil in a large skillet over medium-high heat. Add 4 eggplant rounds and brown them on all sides, about 7 minutes total. Transfer them to a 9-by 13-inch pan. Heat another ¼ cup of oil and repeat with the remaining 4 eggplant rounds. Add them in a single layer to the baking dish.

Heat the remaining 2 tablespoons of oil in the skillet and sauté the onion until soft, about 10 minutes. Add the garlic and sauté until fragrant, about 1 minute. Add the tomatoes, sugar, parsley, thyme, oregano, salt, and pepper, and cook for 15 minutes, stirring occasionally.

Spoon the tomato mixture evenly over the eggplant slices and bake for 30 minutes, or until all the flavors have amalgamated.

This dish is usually served cold or at room temperature. Plate each eggplant slice, squeeze a wedge of lemon over each portion, and serve.

# Orange Galaktoboureko
# (Custard-Filled Phyllo Pastry)

*For most people, Greek dessert means baklava. But if you want to try something differ-*
*ent, make* galaktoboureko. *Growing up as an Orthodox Christian, Dina has enjoyed*
*many Greek Orthodox Church festivals over the years, where the most delicious pastries*
*are baked and sold by church members to support the parish. One of her favorites is this*
*custard-filled phyllo (also spelled filo) pastry soaked in a simple syrup. It is sometimes pre-*
*pared with a lemon-flavored syrup. To make the lemon version, eliminate the orange juice*
*from the custard, and, for the syrup, replace the orange zest and orange juice with lemon*
*zest and lemon juice. You can find boxes of frozen phyllo dough at Greek, Turkish, Middle*
*Eastern, and Armenian stores, and at many supermarkets.*

Makes 20 squares, or enough for 10 servings

2 cups sugar

1 cup water

2 teaspoons orange zest

1 cinnamon stick

1 tablespoon freshly squeezed orange juice (about ⅙ of an orange)

---

4 cups milk

3 eggs

⅓ cup sugar

½ teaspoon ground cinnamon

¼ teaspoon grated nutmeg

½ stick (4 tablespoons) unsalted butter

½ cup farina or cream of wheat

3 tablespoons frozen orange juice concentrate

1 teaspoon pure vanilla extract

---

1 pound frozen phyllo pastry, thawed according to package directions

12 tablespoons (6 ounces) unsalted butter, melted, for brushing phyllo

To make the syrup, mix the sugar, water, orange zest, and cinnamon stick in a medium pot and bring it to a boil. Add the orange juice, reduce the heat, and simmer for 7 minutes. Set the syrup aside to cool. The syrup can be made up to 3 days in advance and kept in the refrigerator until ready to use.

To make the custard, whisk together the milk, eggs, sugar, cinnamon, and nutmeg in a large, heavy pot, until combined. Add the butter and, while whisking frequently, cook over medium-high heat until the butter has melted and the milk has come nearly to a boil. Slowly whisk in the farina until the custard begins to thicken and comes to a boil, about 2 or 3 minutes. Immediately reduce the heat (otherwise it will form big bubbles and splatter) and cook for 1 minute. Remove from the heat and stir in the orange juice concentrate and vanilla. Set aside and cool to room temperature.

Preheat the oven to 400°F.

To prepare the pastry, open the box of phyllo dough and count the sheets. There are usually 20 sheets of phyllo in each packet. Use half for the bottom pastry, half for the top. Place the half that will be used for the top layer under a clean, damp kitchen towel and set aside.

To assemble the galaktoboureko, lay 1 sheet of phyllo on the bottom of a 9- by 13-inch pan, letting the edges hang over the sides. Brush the phyllo on the bottom of the pan with melted butter. Lay another sheet over the first, brush with butter, and continue this way until all the phyllo sheets have been used. Pour the cooled custard over the phyllo.

Cut the remaining phyllo sheets to the size of the pan. One by one, brush each sheet with butter and lay them over the custard. When all the phyllo layers are in place, roll up the overhanging bottom phyllo sheets and tuck them in to seal the custard inside the pastry. Brush the rolled-up phyllo sides and top sheet of phyllo with butter.

With a very sharp knife, carefully score the top layers of phyllo diagonally into diamond shapes. This will help the syrup soak into the pastry and make it easier to cut later on.

Bake for 10 minutes, then reduce the heat to 350°F and bake for 45 minutes, or until golden. Remove the pastry from the oven and let it cool for 5 minutes.

To serve, remove the cinnamon stick from the syrup and pour the cooled syrup over the hot pastry. Cool completely, then cut into squares and serve. Store any extra galaktoboureko, covered with plastic wrap, in the refrigerator for up to 2 days.

# Les Marmitons Cooking Club

Jean-Pierre Jobin got members to join his cooking club by tricking them into it. "I'd offer to buy dinner for my friends, and when they got there, I would tell them we would have to cook it first," laughs Jobin. Les Marmitons is an all-male cooking club, and when Jobin first started to recruit members almost thirty years ago, he says, "It wasn't very popular for men to cook—it was more of a women's thing—but according to tradition, it had to be all men."

Jobin is referring to the traditions of a cooking club that actually dates back to 1950. In the town of Basel, Switzerland, a radio personality and a newspaper man got together with some male friends and started cooking together. The two men began talking about their group on the radio and in the newspaper, and smaller chapters started sprouting up in cities all over Switzerland.

The Knorr Soup Factory heard about these cooking groups and began sponsoring them, sending packages of soup mix and recipes to each of the chapters. In the 1950s, Swiss gas and electric companies had test kitchens where women took cooking classes, and the cooking groups would meet monthly. Knorr supplied the cooking clubs with chef's hats and aprons and wrote about these cooking groups in their newsletters, creating a lot of publicity for the company.

Rene Suter was a member of one of the chapters when he lived in Switzerland, and when he moved to Montreal, he wanted to start a similar cooking group. It took him twelve years to get it started because he could not find a place to hold the gatherings. He loved the original concept of the Swiss groups, and wanted to keep things the same as much as possible. His chef friend, Peter Müller, suggested they ask a cooking school if they could use their facilities, and in 1977, the Montreal chapter of Les Marmitons was born.

The premise for Les Marmitons (*marmitons* is French for a chef's helper or kitchen boy) is simple: The club invites a different professional chef to come to the cooking club each month. The club members cook a five- to seven-course meal, and the guest chef guides and directs them in the preparation of each dish. The chef plans the menu and provides the recipes in advance. Members then shop for the groceries, make copies of the recipes for all the members, and have everything ready the evening the chef arrives for the meeting.

Jobin, an Internet technology consultant, was a member of Les Marmitons in Montreal. He loved the camaraderie of a bunch of guys getting together to cook and drink and learn at the hands of a professional chef. Jobin's job required him to move a lot, and like Suter, he wanted to continue being part of this type of cooking club. So every time he moved, he would start a new chapter of Les Marmitons. Others who heard about Les Marmitons would contact Jobin and ask how to start their own chapter, and Jobin would send them the formal written policies and procedures. As a result, today there are more than thirteen chapters in the United States and Canada with more than seven hundred members.

"I do a lot of sales calls, and as I'm talking to people, the conversation often turns to food and restaurants," says Jobin. "I'll bring up my cooking club, and that's really all it takes. People love the concept, and if they are 'foodies,' they'll ask to join the club by the end of the conversation. Of course, members also realize it is a great networking opportunity to find new friends. Our motto is 'Friendship to Gastronomy,'" he adds. "We have people with all kinds of occupations, from doctors to painters, from bankers to attorneys. Whenever a member needs a service, inevitably one of us knows someone who can help."

Each chapter typically has forty-five or fifty members. Invitations to the monthly cooking club gatherings are done via Evite.com, an online invitation service. The first twenty members to reserve a spot can attend, and meetings usually fill up within ten minutes of the invitations going out, according to Larry Lodisio, a member and past president of the Atlanta chapter. "It's a guys' night out, and you are going to enjoy this great gastronomic feast and some great wine. There's nothing to think about. As soon as you get the invite, you reserve a spot right away if you're available," says Lodisio.

This cooking club format works very well for its members in several ways. They use a professional kitchen instead of cooking in someone's home, and they enjoy learning within that setting. The members cook together and then must speak about the dish they prepared in front of the entire cooking club. "It is very difficult for some people to stand up in front of a group and speak, but it is a great opportunity to learn that skill," says Jobin.

The most obvious benefit to these members, of course, is having a professional chef guide them through the process. "Cooking has become a spectator sport," says Lodisio. "We once had a professional butcher from Ruth's Chris Steak House come in and show us how to butcher our own steak. We all watched and learned and enjoyed each other's company at the same time."

All the members are involved with finding and inviting the chefs. "Most of the time, the chefs have never heard of us. And they don't get paid for coming to our club meetings. But we have been very successful in finding chefs to come teach us, primarily for two reasons: one, it is a great way to bring business and publicity to their restaurant, and two, they appreciate the community service Les Marmitons provides," says Lodisio.

Each chapter offers a variety of fundraising activities to give back to the community. The Atlanta chapter sponsors students from the culinary school where they hold their meetings. "We find people who are having difficulty making ends meet, and we sponsor them to make sure they are able to graduate from this school," says Lodisio.

Once a year, some of the members of the U.S. and Canadian Les Marmitons chapters travel to Calgary, Canada, and choose a cold day in winter to feed more than three thousand people at a homeless shelter. "We feed them breakfast, lunch, and dinner on that day," says Jobin. "It is incredibly rewarding to be involved in something like that, and it all started because of this special cooking club."

## Dames with Flames:
### The Grill of Victory, the Agony of the Heat!

*Let's Get Chillin' and Grillin' Together!*
*We'll Step Away from the Kitchen and Go to the Grill*
*See You on the Patio!*

### Menu

Meyer Lemon and Strawberry Wine Coolers

Bacon-Wrapped Shrimp with Lemon Basil Cream

Caramelized Onion and Clam Dip

Butter Lettuce Salad with Blackberries, Gorgonzola, and Toasted Almonds

Plank-Grilled Quail with Apricot Port Sauce

Creamy Corn Pudding

Grilled Artichokes with Herb Vinaigrette

Peach and Blueberry Crisp

# Meyer Lemon and Strawberry Wine Coolers

*Dina's in-laws, Raul and Anne Guillen, have a Meyer lemon tree growing in their back yard, and every year they give her a generous bag of the most delicious Meyer lemons to take home. Meyers taste somewhat like a cross between a lemon and a mandarin orange. This recipe came about from an afternoon of experimenting with flavors. When Dina serves it to her son and his friends, she leaves out the wine and doubles the water, transforming it from a wine cooler to a delicious strawberry lemonade. If you can't find Meyer lemons, you can substitute regular lemons.*

Makes 8 servings

> 2 cups fresh ripe strawberries, trimmed and cut in half, plus 8 attractive
>    whole strawberries for garnish
> ¼ cup plus 1¼ cups freshly squeezed Meyer (or regular) lemon juice (about
>    5 lemons)
> 1 cup superfine sugar
> 1½ cups water
> 1½ cups white wine, such as Chardonnay or Sauvignon Blanc

Purée the strawberries with the ¼ cup of lemon juice in a blender until smooth. Strain the purée through a fine-mesh sieve into a pitcher and discard the seeds. Add the remaining lemon juice, the sugar, water, and wine to the pitcher and stir until the sugar is dissolved. Adjust sugar to taste. Refrigerate until ready to serve. Serve over ice.

# Bacon-Wrapped Shrimp with Lemon Basil Cream

*This delicious, easy appetizer can be prepared in advance, so you can bring it to your cooking club dinner ready to go whenever the grill is ready. Dina is always looking for tasty dipping sauces to encourage her son Andrew to eat his vegetables, and the Lemon Basil Cream goes perfectly with most any vegetable. It also makes a good dipping sauce for the Grilled Artichokes on page 92.*

Makes 8 servings

8 wooden or bamboo skewers
8 strips bacon
24 jumbo shrimp, shelled and deveined

---

1 cup mayonnaise
¼ cup roughly chopped fresh basil
3 tablespoons freshly squeezed lemon juice (about 1 lemon)
3 cloves garlic, chopped
¼ teaspoon salt
⅛ teaspoon freshly ground black pepper

Soak the skewers in water for 1 hour.

To prepare the shrimp, cut each bacon strip into 3 pieces. Stretch a piece of bacon tightly around the middle of each shrimp and thread the shrimp on a skewer. Repeat with the remaining shrimp and bacon, threading 3 shrimp on each skewer.

Preheat the grill on medium-high heat.

To make the Lemon Basil Cream, combine the mayonnaise, basil, lemon juice, garlic, salt, and pepper in the bowl of a food processor fitted with a steel blade and process until smooth. Set aside.

Grill the wrapped shrimp until they are opaque in the center and the bacon is crispy, about 3 minutes per side. Transfer them to a platter, drizzle with the Lemon Basil Cream, and serve with additional cream on the side for dipping.

# Caramelized Onion and Clam Dip

*We love to entertain, and one of our rules for entertaining is to have as much done before our guests arrive as we can so that we can enjoy their company. This recipe is perfect for parties because it tastes best after it has had a chance to sit and let the flavors blend for awhile. If the chunky texture of chopped clams doesn't appeal to you, minced clams work just as well. Serve the dip with a bountiful platter of fresh vegetable crudités. Our favorites include green or wax beans, blanched asparagus spears, blanched sugar snap peas, red and yellow bell pepper strips, radishes, carrot sticks, zucchini spears, trimmed and grilled scallions, and cherry tomatoes.*

Makes 2 cups or enough for 8 servings

1 tablespoon extra-virgin olive oil
2 medium onions, cut into thin slices
2 teaspoons chopped fresh thyme
Pinch of salt
8 ounces cream cheese, softened
¼ cup sour cream
Two 6.5-ounce cans chopped clams, drained, juices reserved
½ medium-size red bell pepper, finely diced
2 tablespoons freshly squeezed lemon juice (about ⅔ lemon)
½ teaspoon Worcestershire sauce
½ teaspoon seafood seasoning, such as Old Bay
¼ teaspoon cayenne pepper
Salt and freshly ground black pepper

Heat the oil in a large skillet over medium-high heat. Add the onions, thyme, and salt. Lower the heat to medium and sauté, stirring occasionally, for 20 to 25 minutes until onions are caramelized and golden brown. Remove from the heat and let cool.

Combine the cream cheese and sour cream in the bowl of a standing mixer fitted with the whisk attachment. Beat on medium speed until the mixture is smooth and creamy. Stir in the cooled onion mixture, the clams, bell pepper, lemon juice, Worcestershire sauce, seafood seasoning, and cayenne pepper. If the dip seems too thick, add the reserved clam juice, 1 tablespoon at a time, until the desired consistency is achieved. Season with salt and pepper to taste.

Cover the dip and refrigerate until the flavors blend, at least 2 hours or overnight.

# Butter Lettuce Salad with Blackberries, Gorgonzola, and Toasted Almonds

*Dina's husband, Roland, eats pretty healthy and loves green salads with different nuts, fruit, and his favorite cheese, Gorgonzola, mixed in, so she came up with this recipe for him. In summer, when they are in season, try to find sweet, ripe blackberries to balance the tartness of the vinaigrette. Many other fruits also work well, such as blueberries, apples, pears, figs, and peaches.*

Makes 8 servings

⅓ cup extra-virgin olive oil

3 tablespoons sherry vinegar

2 teaspoons honey

2 teaspoons chopped fresh tarragon

½ teaspoon coarse salt

¼ teaspoon freshly ground black pepper

2 heads (about 5 to 6 ounces) butter lettuce, leaves torn into bite-size pieces

1 cup (about 5 ounces) crumbled Gorgonzola cheese

2 cups fresh blackberries

1 cup sliced almonds, toasted

Whisk together the oil, vinegar, honey, tarragon, salt, and pepper in a small bowl. Combine the greens and Gorgonzola in large bowl. Add the dressing and toss well to coat. Evenly divide the greens on 8 salad plates and top with the blackberries and toasted almonds.

# Plank-Grilled Quail with Apricot Port Sauce

*We launched our cookbook-writing career with this very recipe! Dina was hosting a cooking club dinner with a plank-grilling theme. To her surprise, she could not find recipes for anything but salmon, so Dina created this recipe for our gathering. Four of us then began developing other recipes for plank grilling, which evolved into our first cookbook,* The Plank Grilling Cookbook. *If you plan to grill all 16 quail at once, make sure that your grill is big enough to accommodate the two grilling planks. We prefer cedar or alder wood for this recipe, but you can also try maple, cherry, and oak wood—they all offer wonderfully subtle flavor differences. Serve the quail with the Creamy Corn Pudding on page 91. Note: For this recipe, you will need two 7½- by 15- by ⅜-inch grilling planks.*

Makes 8 servings

1 cup red wine, such as Cabernet Sauvignon or Merlot

½ cup extra-virgin olive oil

¼ cup red wine vinegar

¼ cup soy sauce

¼ cup brown sugar

4 cloves garlic, minced

2 bay leaves

1 teaspoon dried thyme

1 teaspoon freshly cracked black pepper

16 fresh or frozen quail (thawed, if frozen)

2 cups ruby port

2 cups chicken broth

½ teaspoon dried thyme

3 tablespoons apricot jam

2 teaspoons Dijon mustard

1 tablespoon plus 1 tablespoon cold unsalted butter

Immerse the grilling planks in water and let them soak for 1 hour or up to overnight.

To make the marinade, put the wine, olive oil, vinegar, soy sauce, brown sugar, garlic, bay, thyme, and pepper in a large bowl. Whisk them together until they are thoroughly combined. Add the quail to the bowl. Mix the quail well with the marinade, making sure they are covered in it. Cover the bowl tightly with plastic wrap and place in the refrigerator. Let the quail marinate for several hours or overnight.

While the quail is marinating and the plank is soaking, prepare the Creamy Corn Pudding on page 91. Put the pudding in the oven about 1 hour before serving the quail.

To make the sauce, put the port, chicken broth, and thyme in a medium-size saucepan and bring it to a boil. Reduce the heat to medium-low and simmer until the liquid has reduced to about $2/3$ cup, about 1 hour. Whisk in the jam and mustard until combined. Remove the pan from the heat and whisk in the butter, 1 tablespoon at a time, until the sauce is emulsified. Set aside.

To cook the quail, prepare the grill and preheat it to medium-high heat, about 425°F. Place the soaked planks on the grill rack, close the lid, and grill for 3 minutes or until they are lightly charred. If the planks are bowed, flip them over and close the grill lid. Continue toasting each side for 1 or 2 minutes until the planks flatten out.

Reduce the heat to medium. Place the quail on the toasted planks and grill for 20 minutes or until the juices run clear. Try to keep the grill lid closed as much as possible, but keep an eye out for flare-ups.

To serve, put a spoonful of corn pudding on each plate. Place 2 quail on top of the corn pudding and drizzle them with the port sauce.

*One of the delights of life is eating with friends; second to that is talking about eating. And, for an unsurpassed double whammy, there is talking about eating while you are eating with friends.*
—Laurie Colwin, *Home Cooking*

## Tips for a Successful
# Grilling Party

- Keep plenty of cold drinks on ice. Chill beverages in a hurry by filling a large, decorative metal tub or other watertight container with bottles of wine and other beverages. Then add a layer of ice, followed by a layer of rock salt; repeat until you almost reach the top. Fill the bucket with cold water just below the ice line. Your drinks will be ice-cold in under 10 minutes.

- Hanging paper lanterns in the trees, from the patio cover, and from patio umbrellas instantly creates a festive atmosphere. No need to put lights in the lanterns. Just hang them up, and you're ready to party.

- To keep your tablecloth from blowing away in the wind, sew tassels from the crafts store around the bottom edges of the cloth. This gives a more finished look, much more elegant than plastic tablecloth clips.

- Fill clear plastic squirt bottles with ketchup, mustard, salad dressings, and so on. Your condiments will look much better this way, and the presentation brings uniformity to the table.

- To keep the bugs away, light some citronella candles. Arrange tiki torches throughout the yard, and have some insect repellant handy for your guests, if necessary. Nothing ruins a party faster than being eaten alive by insects. Caution: Don't use bug sprays around the food or near the grill, candles, or flames.

- Put some of your own secret marinade or barbecue sauce (or your favorite store-bought brand) into small plastic squeeze bottles. Wrap them in butcher paper and tie with a string of raffia ribbon, and give them to your guests as party favors.

# Creamy Corn Pudding

*This pudding's creamy taste and texture will perfectly complement the sweet and succulent flavors of the Plank-Grilled Quail with Apricot Port Sauce on page 88. The recipe calls for baking the pudding in a casserole pan, but if you want to gussy it up a bit, you can make eight individual puddings instead, baking them in little ramekins. Just reduce the baking time to 40 minutes or until the custard sets.*

Makes 12 servings

> 2 tablespoons unsalted butter
> 1 large onion, chopped
> 1 large red bell pepper, chopped
> 4 cloves garlic, minced
> ¼ cup all-purpose flour
> 6 cups fresh corn kernels cut from 10 or 12 ears of corn, any milky liquid reserved
> 4 eggs
> 2 cups heavy cream
> 2 tablespoons sugar
> 2 teaspoons seafood seasoning, such as Old Bay

Preheat the oven to to 350°F.

Melt the butter in a large sauté pan and sauté the onion and bell pepper until softened, about 6 minutes. Add the garlic and sauté for 30 seconds. Add the flour and cook, stirring, for 4 minutes. Pour the mixture into a large bowl and set aside to cool.

Put 4 cups of the corn kernels along with the reserved milky liquid in the bowl of a food processor fitted with a steel blade and process until smooth. Add the puréed corn plus the remaining 2 cups of whole corn kernels to the onion mixture and stir to combine.

In a medium-size bowl, whisk together the eggs, cream, sugar, and seafood seasoning. Add the egg mixture to the corn mixture and stir well to combine.

Pour the mixture into a well-buttered 9- by 13- by 2-inch baking dish. Place the dish inside a larger roasting pan and carefully fill the roasting pan halfway up the sides of the baking dish with hot tap water. Bake the pudding for 50 minutes to 1 hour, or until puffy and golden brown.

# Grilled Artichokes with Herb Vinaigrette

*If you love artichokes, we predict that you will make this recipe over and over again. Marinating the artichokes in an herb vinaigrette, then grilling them to caramelize the sugars, is a great way to prepare this delicious vegetable. The Lemon Basil Cream on page 85 makes a perfect dipping sauce for the artichokes, too.*

Makes 8 servings

8 large artichokes
1 lemon, cut in half
¼ cup plus 1 teaspoon salt

1½ cups extra-virgin olive oil
¾ cup balsamic vinegar
½ cup chopped fresh basil
½ cup chopped fresh parsley
6 cloves garlic, finely chopped
½ teaspoon freshly ground black pepper

To prepare the artichokes, cut the stem flush with the base, and cut off the tight top leaves to remove the prickly tips. With a pair of scissors, trim each side leaf to remove the prickles. Rub the cut parts of the artichokes with the lemon as you work to prevent discoloration.

Put the artichokes in a large pot and add cold water to cover. Add the ¼ cup of salt to the water, then weigh the artichokes down with a heavy dish or bowl. Bring the water to a boil and simmer for about 25 to 30 minutes, or until a paring knife easily pierces the heart of an artichoke. Drain the artichokes upside down and allow them to cool. Cut the cooled artichokes into quarters and scoop out the choke with a spoon. Set the artichokes aside.

To make the herb vinaigrette, combine the oil, vinegar, basil, parsley, garlic, pepper, and the remaining teaspoon of salt in a large bowl. Add the artichoke quarters and toss to coat. Let the artichokes marinate for 1 hour.

Prepare and heat the grill to medium-high heat. Remove the artichokes from the bowl, reserving the vinaigrette. Grill the artichokes until they are lightly charred, about 3 minutes per side. Arrange them on a platter, and pour the reserved herb vinaigrette over the artichokes.

# Peach and Blueberry Crisp

*Fruit desserts are Dina's favorites. She is a sucker for fruit cobblers, fruit pies, fruit crostatas, and, most especially, for fruit crisps. Peaches and blueberries are a perfect match in this crisp, and the gingersnap crumbles are a nice twist on a classic recipe. Make sure you have some good-quality vanilla bean ice cream on hand to serve with this crisp.*

Makes 8 servings

6 ripe peaches (about 2 pounds)
1 cup fresh or frozen blueberries (thawed if frozen)
½ cup sugar
2 tablespoons all-purpose flour
2 teaspoons lemon zest
2 tablespoons freshly squeezed lemon juice (about ⅔ lemon)
½ teaspoon ground cinnamon

¾ cup all-purpose flour
½ cup coarsely crushed gingersnaps
¼ cup chopped walnuts
2 tablespoons light brown sugar
2 tablespoons granulated sugar
½ teaspoon ground cinnamon
¼ teaspoon salt
7 tablespoons cold unsalted butter, cut into ½-inch dice

1 pint vanilla-bean ice cream (optional)

Preheat the oven to 350°F. Butter an 8- by 8- by 2½-inch square baking dish.

To make the filling, fill a large bowl with cold water. Fill a medium-size saucepan with water and bring it to a boil. Cut an "X" in the end opposite the stem of each peach. Immerse the peaches in the boiling water for 30 seconds, then immediately put them in the cold water for 2 minutes. Discard the water and set the bowl aside. Peel the peaches, cut them into thick wedges, and put them in the bowl. Add the blueberries, sugar, flour, zest, lemon juice, and cinnamon and mix gently. Transfer to the prepared baking dish.

To make the topping, put the flour, gingersnaps, walnuts, brown sugar, granulated sugar, cinnamon, salt, and butter into the bowl of a standing mixer fitted with the paddle attachment. Mix on low speed just until the mixture resembles coarse meal, about 1 or 2 minutes. Sprinkle the topping evenly over the fruit.

Set the baking dish on top of a sheet pan and bake for 45 minutes, or until the topping is golden brown. Cool for at least 20 minutes. To serve, spoon the warm crisp into bowls. Top each portion with a scoop of ice cream, if desired.

# The Outdoor Adventure Social Club

Cliffs, caves, and kayaks are common vehicles for fun and adventure to the members of the Outdoor Adventure Social Club (OASC) of Charlottesville, Virginia. The club, which recently topped 230 members ranging in age from twenty- to sixty-something, offers residents of Charlottesville an opportunity to get together and share the breathtaking scenery and wilderness adventures their community offers.

But not every activity leads to spelunking, white-water rafting, rock climbing, rappelling, or mountain biking. Margie Danner-Roth heads the OASC cooking club, where members who have an interest in cooking can gather at each other's homes and learn to cook. "It's a great group of people with a good mix of men and women," says Danner-Roth. "One day we'll be kayaking down the James River, the next day we'll be preparing shrimp étouffée together."

Danner-Roth says OASC members have some fundamental common interests. "We love life, we obviously love adventure and exploring, and we love different cultures. Cooking is a great way to explore those common interests further," says Danner-Roth.

As leader of the group, Danner-Roth is responsible for finding places to meet, planning and posting the menu each month, taking RSVPs, and purchasing the groceries (members pay their share to cover costs). The club meets at a member's home and splits up into groups. Each group tackles a dish together. They typically have about ninety minutes to get the food prepped, cooked, and on the table.

According to Danner-Roth, there are usually eight to ten people at each cooking club gathering. She believes menu planning is the most important part of her job. "When I planned an American-themed dinner menu, hardly anyone wanted to come. Whenever I plan an exotic theme, there are so many RSVPs I have to start a waiting list. It's all about the menu," Danner-Roth says.

Themes have ranged from New Orleans cuisine to Cuban, Mediterranean, and Hawaiian. And no matter what the theme, Danner-Roth says she always includes a vegetarian dish on the menu.

Danner-Roth says she enjoys all the spices and seasonings she has been exposed to as a result of exploring different cuisines. "I find myself choosing a recipe based primarily on how long it takes to make, since we have a short amount of time to prep and cook. Then I look at the seasonings involved; it has been a great education learning about spices I'd never even heard of before," she says.

Since Danner-Roth is responsible for ensuring that her cooking club has a menu, recipes, and groceries before they meet, she has one major piece of advice for anyone who wants to start a cooking club: read the recipe all the way through before putting it on the menu. "I look to make sure that it can be prepared in the time we have, although I will do certain things, like marinate meat, before the group meets. And I try to make sure it is a good recipe. We haven't had too many flops, but the ones we did have were doozies," she adds. She describes an instance during the New Orleans–themed gathering where the bread pudding never set and the custard had a liquid consistency after baking. "We just drank it," Danner-Roth laughs.

"It's all about getting together with friends, having a wonderful time sharing something we enjoy immensely. That's what's important," says Danner-Roth. "This group has been a godsend to me, and I look forward to our gatherings every time."

*Mangia!*

*You Are Cordially Invited to One Big Italian Dinner Party*

*With Dishes Just Like Nonna Used to Make*

*Buon Appetito!*

### *Menu*

Limoncello Coolers

Mamma Mary Garayalde's Antipasto Platter

Enrichetta's Stuffed Calamari

Rosemary Focaccia Bread

Pollo Toscano

Risotto con Parmigiano-Reggiano

Roasted Asparagus with Portobello Mushrooms
and Parmigiano-Reggiano

Affogato

# Limoncello Coolers

*Ever since Danny DeVito showed up half in the bag on* The View *from one too many limon-cellos the night before, we've wanted to try one for ourselves. Limoncello, a liqueur made from lemon peel, alcohol, and sugar, is served as an after-dinner digestivo all over Italy. For cooking club, we served it over ice with some club soda. These coolers are light, refreshing, and go down way too easy, so be careful. As Danny DeVito said, "I knew it was the seventh limoncello that was going to get me!"*

Makes 8 coolers

>     4 cups crushed ice
>     4 cups limoncello
>     8 tablespoons freshly squeezed lemon juice (about 2⅔ lemons)
>     2 cups fresh mint leaves
>     2 cups club soda, chilled
>     1 lemon cut into 8 slices
>     8 sprigs fresh mint

Fill 8 tall, skinny glasses halfway with crushed ice. To each glass, add ½ cup limoncello, 1 tablespoon lemon juice, and ¼ cup of the mint leaves. Muddle with the back of a wooden spoon, crushing the mint leaves well. Slowly add ¼ cup club soda to each glass and garnish with a lemon slice and a sprig of mint.

# Mamma Mary Garayalde's Antipasto Platter

*Michelle's dear Italian friend Bonnie Bussard was kind enough to give us this wonderful antipasto recipe, and we consider it an honor that Bonnie's mother, Mary Garayalde, was willing to share it. This dish was one of the seven seafood dishes that Mary and her hus-band, John, served for the traditional Christmas Eve Feast of the Seven Fishes. The platter makes a perfect first course for entertaining your cooking club.*

Makes 10 servings

>     Two 12-ounce cans oil-packed albacore tuna, drained
>     One 14.5-ounce jar marinated artichoke hearts, drained
>     One 4-ounce jar nonpareil capers, drained

One 15-ounce can garbanzo beans, drained, rinsed well

One 15-ounce can red kidney beans, drained, rinsed well

One 16-ounce jar *peperoncini* peppers, stems left intact, ½ cup liquid
    reserved for dressing

One 16-ounce jar Italian-style mixed pickled vegetables (*giardiniera*), ½ cup
    liquid reserved for dressing

One 6-ounce can black olives, drained

One 7-ounce jar pitted green olives, drained

1 small white onion, finely diced

One 8-ounce can tomato sauce

---

3 tablespoons extra-virgin olive oil

2 tablespoons white distilled vinegar

½ teaspoon dried parsley flakes

½ teaspoon garlic powder

½ teaspoon dried oregano

To make the antipasto, combine the tuna, artichoke hearts, capers, garbanzo beans, kidney beans, peperoncini, pickled vegetables, olives, onion, and tomato sauce in a large bowl.

To make the dressing, in a small bowl, whisk together the oil, vinegar, and the reserved liquid from the peppers and the pickled vegetables. Add the parsley, garlic, and oregano and whisk to combine. Pour the dressing over the antipasto and mix until thoroughly combined. Cover the bowl with plastic wrap and refrigerate overnight or for at least 6 hours before serving. To serve, transfer the antipasto to a large, attractive serving platter.

# Enrichetta's Stuffed Calamari

*When Michelle's friend Bonnie Bussard shared this recipe with us, we knew it had to be included in this cookbook. This is Bonnie's grandmother Enrichetta's recipe, and is prepared for the family's Christmas Eve feast. This dish has been passed down through her family, and Bonnie will no doubt teach this to her two beautiful daughters, Ashley and Haley, as well. This recipe will surely dirty a few pans, but the result is well worth it. See the boxed tip for detailed directions on cleaning squid.*

Makes 10 servings

10 squid, each body 5 to 6 inches long, with tentacles removed and
  reserved, cleaned and rinsed (see sidebar on page 104)

2 tablespoons plus ½ cup extra-virgin olive oil
One 15-ounce can stewed tomatoes, puréed in blender or food processor
4 cloves garlic, chopped
1 small white onion, finely chopped
10 fresh basil leaves, finely chopped
2 teaspoons dried oregano
salt and pepper

15 ounces ricotta cheese
1 large egg
½ cup freshly grated Parmesan cheese
1 teaspoon dried Italian parsley
1 teaspoon salt
¼ teaspoon freshly ground black pepper
10 wooden toothpicks

1 cup all-purpose flour, seasoned with salt and pepper
¼ cup dry white wine

To prepare the squid tentacles, put them in a medium-size pot of boiling salted water. Lower the heat to a simmer. Simmer the tentacles, covered, over medium heat for 15 to 20 minutes or until tender. Drain the tentacles and allow them to cool. Once the tentacles have cooled, chop fine.

To make the tomato sauce, in a large sauté pan, heat the 2 tablespoons olive oil over medium heat. Add the tomatoes, garlic, onion, basil, and oregano. Simmer, uncovered, for 20 minutes. Adjust the sauce for seasoning, adding salt and pepper if desired. Set aside.

To prepare the filling, in a large bowl, mix together the ricotta, tentacles, egg, Parmesan, parsley, salt, and pepper. Stuff each squid body with about 1 heaping teaspoon of the cheese mixture. Use more or less filling depending on the size of the squid. With a toothpick, close up the end of the squid body. Do not be tempted to overstuff the squid; you should be able to easily close the ends with the toothpick.

Preheat the oven to 400°F.

To cook the squid, put the seasoned flour on a large plate and dredge the squid, making sure to coat them well with flour. Heat the ½ cup of oil in a large skillet over medium heat and sauté the squid until they are browned on all sides, about 2 minutes per side. Unless your skillet is big enough to accommodate all of the squid at once, you will have to cook them in batches. Cover the first batch loosely with aluminum foil while cooking the second batch.

Drain the oil from the skillet and deglaze the pan by pouring the white wine into the pan and scraping up any brown bits. Allow the wine to come to a boil for 1 minute to concentrate the flavors. Add the reserved tomato sauce mixture to the deglazed pan and heat it for 3 minutes over medium heat. Arrange the squid in a roasting pan and pour the tomato sauce evenly over the squid. Cover the pan tightly with aluminum foil and bake for 45 minutes until the squid is tender and opaque. Remove the toothpicks from the squid and arrange decoratively on a serving platter.

## HOW TO CLEAN SQUID

Grab the body of the squid in one hand and the head (tentacles) in the other, and, with a slight twisting motion, pull apart the two sections. The edible parts are the body and the tentacles. With a knife, cut just below the eyes, cutting straight down to remove the innards and the head, leaving the tentacles behind. Next, remove and discard the thin, clear piece of cartilage from inside the body by grasping the tail and pulling. Next, remove the outer skin by grasping an exposed edge of skin and pulling it back away from the flesh of the body. Clean the body and the tentacles well with cold running water, rinsing the inside of the body as well.

# Rosemary Focaccia Bread

*Baking bread from scratch has always amazed us. Bread at its most basic is nothing more than flour and water, and that simple recipe has sustained life since the beginnings of time. This wonderful focaccia is fluffy and chewy and is the perfect complement to any Italian meal.*

Makes 1 large focaccia sheet or enough for 8 servings

> 2 cups lukewarm water (105°F to 115°F)
> ¼ ounce active dry yeast
> 5 cups plus ½ cup all-purpose flour, as needed
> ¼ cup plus 5 tablespoons extra-virgin olive oil
> 2 teaspoons plus 2 teaspoons coarse sea salt
> 2 tablespoons finely chopped fresh rosemary

In the bowl of an electric mixer fitted with the dough hook attachment, stir together the water and yeast. Let the mixture stand until the yeast has completely dissolved, about 10 minutes.

To the yeast mixture, add the 5 cups of flour, the ¼ cup of oil, and the 2 teaspoons of salt. Mix on low speed until soft and thoroughly combined, about 2 minutes. The dough will be quite sticky.

Turn the dough out onto a lightly floured work surface and knead in additional flour by the tablespoon as needed (up to ½ cup depending on the weather), until the dough is still sticky but not wet. Transfer the dough to a large bowl that has been lightly oiled. Cover the bowl with a clean, damp towel. Put the bowl in a warm place away from any drafts and let the dough rise for 1 hour or until it has doubled in size.

Press the dough into an oiled 15- by 10-inch rimmed baking sheet and cover with plastic wrap. Let the dough rise for an hour.

Preheat the oven to 500°F.

Stir together the remaining 5 tablespoons of oil and the rosemary in a small bowl. Pressing lightly with your fingertips, make shallow indentations all over the dough. Drizzle the oil mixture over the dough and sprinkle with the remaining 2 teaspoons of salt. If the salt seems too coarse, crush it lightly with your fingers before sprinkling.

Bake the focaccia for 5 minutes, then lower the heat to 475°F for 10 to 12 minutes, or until the focaccia is golden brown. Flip the focaccia onto a rack to cool 20 to 25 minutes before serving.

# Pollo Toscano

*For a birthday celebration that Dina threw for fellow cooking club member Cindy LaCasse, Michelle brought this dish, and it received raves. You can substitute any other kind of good-quality brined black olives for the kalamatas in this recipe. The chicken needs to marinate overnight to maximize the flavor, so plan accordingly.*

1½ cups full-bodied red wine such as Petite Syrah or Zinfandel

6 celery stalks, cut into ½-inch cubes

1 large yellow onion, finely chopped

15 whole cloves garlic, peeled

30 large black kalamata olives, pitted and drained

1 cup golden raisins

1 cup capers, drained

1 tablespoon herbes de Provence

2 bay leaves

2 teaspoons salt

½ teaspoon freshly ground black pepper

16 bone-in, skin-on chicken thighs (about 5 pounds)

2 tablespoons extra-virgin olive oil

2 cups beef stock, preferably homemade

½ cup tomato paste

In a large sauté pan set over high heat, combine the wine, celery, onion, garlic, olives, raisins, capers, herbes de Provence, bay leaves, salt, and pepper. Allow the mixture to come to a boil, then reduce the temperature to medium. Stirring occasionally, simmer the marinade for 10 to 15 minutes or until the marinade has thickened slightly. Remove the pan from the heat, cover, and allow the mixture to cool to room temperature. Transfer the cooled marinade and the chicken thighs to a large bowl. Cover the bowl with plastic wrap and put it in the refrigerator for 4 hours or overnight to allow the flavors to blend.

Preheat the oven to 350°F.

Remove the chicken from the marinade; reserve the marinade for later use. Heat the oil in a large skillet over medium heat. Sauté the chicken thighs on each side until they are golden brown and the skin is crisp, about 5 minutes per side.

You will need to work in batches if your pan is not big enough to cook all the chicken at once.

To the reserved marinade, add the beef stock and tomato paste, mixing well to combine. Place the pan over high heat, bring to a boil, and cook for 15 minutes until reduced slightly. Transfer the chicken pieces to a large baking dish big enough to accommodate the chicken in a single layer, and pour the sauce evenly over the chicken. Bake the chicken for 45 minutes until juices run clear.

Degrease the chicken by carefully skimming off any accumulated fat with a large metal spoon. Remove the bay leaves and transfer the chicken and sauce to a serving platter. Serve the chicken and sauce alongside the Risotto con Parmigiano-Reggiano on page 108.

# Risotto con Parmigiano-Reggiano

*Michelle's husband, Corey, loves risotto, and 9 times out of 10, if he sees it on a menu he will order it. This dish is a classic, and it is meant to be served alongside the Pollo Toscano on page 106. Risotto needs to be stirred continually, so don't leave it on the stove unattended. If you prepare your cooking club dishes at your home, make the risotto all the way up until the last cup of broth is needed, then finish the dish in the host's kitchen, incorporating the last amount of broth and the cheese just before serving.*

Makes 8 side-dish servings

> 5 cups chicken stock, preferably homemade
> ½ cup dry white wine such as Sauvignon Blanc or Chardonnay
> 2 tablespoons plus 2 tablespoons unsalted butter
> 4 large shallots, finely minced
> 4 cloves garlic, finely minced
> 1½ cups arborio rice
> ¾ cup grated plus 1 tablespoon shaved Parmigiano-Reggiano cheese
> 1 tablespoon chopped fresh flat-leaf parsley
> 1 teaspoon salt
> ¼ teaspoon freshly ground black pepper
> 1 tablespoon balsamic vinegar

Bring the stock and wine to a boil in a medium-size saucepan. Cover the pan and reduce the heat to low.

In a heavy medium-size saucepan, melt 2 tablespoons of the butter over medium-low heat. Add the shallots and garlic and sauté until tender but not brown, about 8 to 10 minutes. Increase the heat to medium and add the rice. Cook the rice, stirring occasionally, for about 3 minutes to lightly toast. Add 1½ cups of the hot stock mixture, stirring continually, and let the rice mixture simmer until the liquid is just absorbed. Add another cup of stock and stir until the liquid is just absorbed. Add remaining 2½ cups of broth, ½ cup at a time, stirring continually, until the liquid is absorbed and the rice is creamy and tender, about 35 minutes. Remove the pan from the heat.

Add the grated cheese, parsley, the remaining 2 tablespoons of butter, the salt, and pepper, and mix well. Just before serving, garnish the risotto with the shavings of cheese and a drizzle of balsamic vinegar.

# Roasted Asparagus with Portobello Mushrooms and Parmigiano-Reggiano

*For this recipe, the roasted asparagus becomes caramelized and golden brown, and it looks beautiful turned out onto a nice platter. Italian cooking is all about using simple, fresh ingredients at the peak of their flavors, and this easy but delicious recipe makes both the asparagus and the portobello mushrooms shine.*

Makes 8 servings

> 1 pound portobello mushrooms, thinly sliced
> ½ cup extra-virgin olive oil
> 6 cloves garlic, chopped
> 2 teaspoons fresh rosemary, chopped
> 2 teaspoons fresh thyme, chopped
> 1 pound asparagus, stems trimmed, cut into 2-inch pieces
> 1 tablespoon balsamic vinegar
> ¼ cup shaved Parmigiano-Reggiano cheese

Preheat the oven to 375°F.

Put the mushrooms in a large baking dish and set aside. Put the olive oil, garlic, rosemary, and thyme in a small bowl and mix well. Pour the oil mixture over the mushrooms, stirring well to combine.

Bake the mushrooms for 10 minutes. Add the asparagus to the mushrooms, mixing well to make sure the oil coats the asparagus, and cook for another 10 minutes, or until the asparagus is cooked through. Remove the dish from the oven, and just before serving, drizzle with the balsamic vinegar and the Parmigiano-Reggiano.

*The trouble with eating Italian food is that five or six days later you're hungry again.*
—George Miller

### Tips for a Successful
# Italian-Inspired Dinner

- To us, no tribute to Italian food would be complete without Frank Sinatra or Tony Bennett crooning in the background, or perhaps an Italian opera is more to your liking.

- To evoke an old-school Italian restaurant, put a red and white checkered tablecloth on the table, topped with a raffia-covered Chianti bottle with a candle in it. Make sure the bottle has plenty of dripping wax on it.

- Host a *Godfather* or *Sopranos* party, and invite your guests to dress up as one of their favorite characters. Invitations might read, "You are invited to a party you can't refuse."

- For a rustic setting, dine at a natural wood table with mismatched plates and cutlery. Use short juice tumblers for wine glasses.

- Hang bunches of dried herbs overhead or from the backs of chairs.

- Place wildflowers in big bunches around the table for a charming, natural touch.

- Use the colors of the Italian flag for the place settings. Set off a simple white tablecloth with red plates and a green table runner.

- Host a *Cinema Paradiso* party. Put the dining table and chairs in the backyard, hang up an old white sheet for a movie curtain, and screen vintage Italian movies on it. Ask your guests to bring their favorites and watch them during dessert.

# Affogato

*Affogato is gelato with espresso poured over it, and in Italian it literally means "drowned." For cooking club, prepare the espresso ahead of time and reheat just before serving. Beat the cream at the last minute, as cream that is beaten too early will separate.*

Makes 8 servings

1 cup cold heavy cream
2 tablespoons confectioners' sugar
1 teaspoon pure vanilla extract

2 cups boiling water
3 tablespoons instant espresso powder, regular or decaffeinated
2 pints vanilla gelato
8 tablespoons Kahlúa liqueur
Toasted slivered almonds, for garnish

Beat the cream with an electric hand mixer or standing mixer until soft peaks form. Add the sugar and vanilla and mix until just combined.

In a small bowl, whisk together the boiling water and the espresso powder until well combined. Put 2 small scoops of gelato in each of 8 dessert cups, and top the gelato with ¼ cup of the hot espresso and 1 tablespoon of the Kahlúa. Garnish with the whipped cream and slivered almonds. Serve immediately.

# The Nashville Wine.Dine.Donate Cooking Club

"I think entertaining people in your own home is a dying art," says Susan Goodwin of Nashville, Tennessee. "People get intimidated about cooking and entertaining, so they just go to a restaurant." Goodwin had been thinking a long time about starting her own cooking club where she could cook and entertain in her own home with others. She had recently returned from a cooking tour in Italy when she saw a full-page advertisement in *Gourmet* magazine about a program called Wine.Dine.Donate. "I went on the Epicurious.com Web site and read about the program. That was the catalyst for me."

Wine.Dine.Donate is a program developed by Epicurious.com to help end hunger in America. Every month, Epicurious features new menus and recipes developed by America's top chefs. Everyone is encouraged to host dinner parties using those menus and to ask guests to donate money to America's Second Harvest, the nation's largest network of food banks, or to their local food bank. Epicurious provides tips and timelines; a link to sources for ingredients, wines, and equipment; an online forum for sharing experiences and photos of the event; and a downloadable tool kit with invitations, place cards, and menus.

"I loved some of those chef-inspired menus, but I like to plan my own menus, so I didn't use that part of the program," says Goodwin. She immediately began the Nashville chapter of Wine.Dine.Donate by sending e-mails to her friends and co-workers, inviting them to a dinner party that she was hosting. She asked everyone who wanted to attend to give a minimum donation of twenty-five dollars, "or whatever they would spend at a nice restaurant if they were going out to dinner."

Goodwin planned her menu based on her trip to Italy, with dishes from the Cinque Terre (in the Liguria region of northern Italy). "I prepared the whole thing," she says. "I asked people to come and enjoy the food and wine, and in lieu of bringing food or drinks, to write out a check to our local food bank, the Second Harvest Food Bank."

That was in September 2006, and her cooking club has been going strong ever since. They have raised about three hundred dollars at each dinner, and each gathering is usually booked within minutes of an email invitation being sent, after which a waiting list is created in case someone needs to cancel. "I sent out an e-mail at the end of the first year asking if everyone wanted to continue, and to ask for hosts for the upcoming year, and there were so many people who signed up that we filled the host list within a day or two," says Goodwin. She has since arranged it so that people could team up, so everyone who wants to host can have the opportunity.

The cooking club has over thirty members, but typically a group of about eight to thirteen people can attend each cooking club gathering. "That's about all we can handle in each person's home," says Goodwin. "We have learned every aspect of throwing a five- to eight-course gourmet dinner together for a large group of people and how to be comfortable with that experience," she adds.

Learning how to entertain was important for Goodwin because she saw her parents benefit from the experience. "They have been in a cooking club for over thirty years, and they have a solid social network of friends as a result of their cooking club. I wanted the same for myself," she says.

When asked if her cooking club has any rules or guidelines they follow, Goodwin replies, "You have to have a stomach to enjoy the food, a mouth to socialize with others, and a checkbook to donate." Her group likes to keep things flexible, with as few rules as possible.

Goodwin has been the coordinator of the group since its inception, and she encourages people who want to start a similarly styled cooking club to make sure that a coordinator is in place. "The hosts pick a date, plan the menu, and do the cooking, but as the coordinator, I make sure everyone gets the menu, I keep track of the RSVPs, I collect the checks, and I make sure the food bank receives the money."

Being a part of a cooking club like this is a lot of work, but Goodwin says that what keeps them going is a combination of motivations. "People feel really good about donating to a food bank. I mean, what we are doing is going to end up feeding a lot of kids who would otherwise go to bed hungry; what's not to love about that?" Add to that the opportunity to make good friends, learn to cook gourmet meals, and become proficient at entertaining in your own home, and Goodwin says this is one of the most rewarding experiences she has ever been involved in.

# Hawaiian Luau:
## From Pig to Poi

*Aloha, Friends!*

*The Pineapple Martinis Are Ready and the Time Is Set*

*Get Ready for a Luau You'll Not Soon Forget!*

## Menu

Pineapple-Sunset Martinis

Hawaiian Macadamia Nut Muffins

Taste of the Islands Chicken Wings

Seared Ahi Tuna Tacos with Hawaiian Slaw

Hearts of Palm, Mandarin Orange, and Avocado Salad with Poi Vinaigrette

Kalua Pork

Aloha Shrimp with Pineapple Fried Rice

Macadamia Nut Pie with Creamy Coconut Ice Cream

# Pineapple-Sunset Martinis

*Pineapples are an integral part of Hawaiian cuisine, and it seems only fitting that the pineapple, a symbol of hospitality, be featured in the cocktail with which you will welcome your guests. This sweet drink goes down easy and can be deceptively dangerous—consider yourself warned. The mixture needs to mellow in the fridge for at least 10 days, so be sure to plan ahead.*

Makes 15 martinis

> 1 liter premium vodka
> 2 large ripe pineapples, cored, peeled, and cut into 1-inch chunks
> 2 ounces grenadine syrup

In a large glass container, combine the vodka and the pineapple chunks, cover, and allow them to macerate in the refrigerator for 10 days. After 10 days, if the vodka does not seem sweet enough, allow the mixture to macerate for up to 3 weeks. Check it daily, until it has reached your desired level of sweetness.

When the mixture is sweet enough, strain it through a fine sieve, reserving 15 of the pineapple cubes. Put the mixture back into refrigerator to keep it well chilled until just before serving. Mixture can be stored up to 6 weeks.

To prepare 1 cocktail, pour ¼ cup of the pineapple mixture into a chilled martini glass. Slowly add a dash (6 drops) of grenadine, allowing it to settle to the bottom. Garnish the glass with a pineapple cube. Repeat for each drink.


# Hawaiian Macadamia Nut Muffins

*These muffins were inspired by CJ's, a little bakery and deli where Michelle and her husband, Corey, stopped to buy a picnic lunch for their drive out to Hana, on the back side of Maui. CJ's made one of the best muffins Michelle has ever had, and she's done her best to recreate it. These little gems have just the right amount of sweetness and are a natural accompaniment to a Hawaiian-inspired menu.*

Makes 10 muffins

½ cup vegetable oil

2 large ripe bananas, mashed

1 cup roasted macadamia nuts, coarsely chopped

2 eggs

1¼ cups all-purpose flour

¾ cup sugar

1 teaspoon baking powder

½ teaspoon salt

Preheat the oven to 375°F.

Butter 10 cups of a 12-cup muffin pan, or line the cups with paper liners. In a large bowl, combine the oil, bananas, nuts, and eggs, stirring until thoroughly blended. Sift together the flour, sugar, baking powder, and salt, and stir them into the banana mixture, mixing until just combined. Fill the muffin cups almost to the top. Bake the muffins for 20 minutes or until golden brown and a toothpick placed in the center of the muffin comes out clean. Slightly cool the muffins on a wire rack before serving. Serve warm.

# Taste of the Islands Chicken Wings

*We love chicken wings; they are messy, tasty, and just plain fun to eat. These island-inspired wings look great turned out on a big platter and served communal style, or should we say island style? They need to marinate for a day in your fridge, so make sure you plan accordingly.*

Makes 24 wings or enough for 8 servings

1 cup pineapple juice

½ cup soy sauce

4 cloves garlic, minced

1 teaspoon grated fresh gingerroot

¼ teaspoon freshly ground black pepper

4 pounds chicken wings (about 20 to 24 wings), wing tips removed

2 scallions, chopped

In a medium-size bowl, combine the pineapple juice, soy sauce, garlic, ginger, and pepper and mix thoroughly. Put the chicken wings in a large container and pour the marinade over the wings, tossing well to coat. Cover tightly with a lid or plastic wrap and put the wings in the refrigerator for at least 6 hours and up to 24 hours.

Preheat the oven to 375°F.

Put the wings with the marinade in a large roasting pan and cook, uncovered, for 1 hour, or until wings are browned and juices run clear. Garnish with the scallions.

# Seared Ahi Tuna Tacos with Hawaiian Slaw

*These are no ordinary tacos. This recipe uses crispy wonton wrappers instead of taco shells for a whimsical twist on the Mexican standard. The seared ahi is seasoned with* shichimi togarashi, *a spice mix commonly used in Japanese cooking. It can be found in most Asian markets in the spice aisle, or you can order it online. If you serve these tacos as an appetizer, along with the Pineapple-Sunset Martinis, your fellow club members will be doing the hula for sure. To serve, arrange the tacos in the center of a platter surrounded by the extra slaw.*

Makes 16 tacos or enough for 8 servings

> 4 tablespoons extra-virgin olive oil
> 1 pound sushi-grade ahi tuna, cut into 4 pieces, about 6 inches long and ¼ inch thick
> 2 tablespoons *shichimi togarashi*
> 1 teaspoon salt
> About 6 cups vegetable oil for frying
> 16 round wonton wrappers
> Hawaiian Slaw (recipe follows)
> Fresh cilantro sprigs for garnish

In a large skillet set over medium-high heat, heat the olive oil until shimmering and hot. Sprinkle the tuna liberally with the shichimi togarashi and the salt, pressing the seasoning into the fish. Sear the tuna in the hot oil on all sides for 8 to 10 seconds. Remove the tuna from the pan and allow to cool, then cut each of the 4 pieces into 6 slices with a sharp knife. Set aside.

Heat 1 inch of vegetable oil in a large skillet over high heat until the oil reaches 350°F. With a pair of tongs, hold a wonton wrapper, folding it over so it forms a U-shaped shell. Place it carefully in the hot oil. Fry each wonton for about 1 minute, or until the wrapper is crispy and golden, then let them drain on paper towels.

To assemble the tacos, place 1 tablespoon of the prepared Hawaiian Slaw into each shell and top it with 3 slices of the tuna. Garnish with sprigs of cilantro.

## Hawaiian Slaw
Makes 4 cups or enough for 8 servings

> 3 tablespoons rice wine vinegar
> 2 tablespoons sesame oil
> 1 tablespoon soy sauce
> 1 tablespoon light brown sugar
> 1 tablespoon shredded sweetened coconut
> 2 teaspoons grated fresh gingerroot
> 3 cloves garlic, minced
> 2 teaspoons crunchy-style peanut butter
> 1 shallot, finely minced
> 1 medium head (4 cups) very finely shredded cabbage

In a small bowl, whisk together the vinegar, oil, soy sauce, brown sugar, coconut, ginger, garlic, peanut butter, and shallot. Set aside. Put the shredded cabbage and the dressing in a medium-size bowl and combine thoroughly. The dressing can be made up to a day ahead, then tossed with the cabbage just before serving.

# Hearts of Palm, Mandarin Orange, and Avocado Salad with Poi Vinaigrette

*This recipe has everything you could want in a salad: it's sweet, it's salty, and it's very refreshing. The Poi Vinaigrette gives this salad a Hawaiian flavor that is not overpowering. Hearts of palm are taken from the inner core of the palm tree; harvesting is very labor intensive, thus they can be a little pricey, and they are considered a delicacy by many. They're delicious in a salad, but we love to eat them straight out of the can, too. This recipe has several parts, so first cook the poi, then prepare the vinaigrette, and last of all, make the hearts of palm salad. Maybe it's a bit of a production, but it's worth it. If you don't want to make the poi vinaigrette, this salad tastes great topped with an Asian-style dressing.*

Makes 8 servings

> Two 14-ounce cans hearts of palm, drained
> 2 California avocados, firm but ripe
> 1 tablespoon lemon juice (about ½ small lemon)
> Poi Vinaigrette (recipe follows)
> 2 heads butter lettuce, leaves separated from the heads, washed and dried
> One 11-ounce can mandarin oranges, drained
> ½ sweet Maui or Vidalia onion, cut into ¼-inch thick rings

Cut the hearts of palm and the avocados into 1-inch pieces and put them in a large bowl. Add the lemon juice and toss gently. Add the Poi Vinaigrette and gently toss until just combined.

To serve, arrange the lettuce leaves on 8 salad plates or 1 large serving platter, and spoon the hearts of palm mixture over the lettuce leaves. Arrange the mandarin orange slices and onion rings decoratively over the salad and serve immediately.

## Poi Vinaigrette

Makes ¼ cup or enough for 8 servings

> 2 tablespoons Mashed Poi
> 1 tablespoon rice wine vinegar
> 2 cloves garlic, minced
> 2 teaspoons Dijon mustard

½ teaspoon soy sauce

3 sprigs fresh cilantro, stems removed

2 tablespoons vegetable oil

Put the poi, vinegar, garlic, mustard, soy sauce, and cilantro in a blender jar and pulse until just combined. Still pulsing, add the oil in a slow stream until the dressing is emulsified. Refrigerate the dressing until ready to serve.

## Mashed Poi

Makes 1 cup or enough for 8 servings

8 ounces taro root, peeled and cut into ½-inch cubes

Water, as needed

Put the taro root into a medium-size saucepan over high heat. Add enough water to cover the taro and allow it to come to a boil. Turn down the heat to medium and simmer for 30 to 35 minutes, or until the taro is easily pierced with a fork. The taro should be soft but not mushy. Drain the taro and transfer it to a medium-size bowl.

While still hot, mash the taro with a potato masher and add water, 1 tablespoon at a time, until it reaches the consistency of mashed potatoes. Mash until there are very few lumps. (A few lumps are okay, but as it will be used in the vinaigrette dressing, it should be as smooth as possible. Scoop out any bigger lumps and discard them before serving.) Serve any extra poi alongside Kalua Pork on page 122.

### POI PRAGMATICS

When Michelle first made poi for cooking club, she was a little unsure of herself, so she cooked up a practice batch—and she was glad she did. Unbeknownst to her, if you don't cook the taro root long enough, it can irritate the heck out of your throat. For the rest of the day, her throat felt like it had been scrubbed with sandpaper. She was so glad she hadn't served that poi to her cooking club. Taro root contains calcium chloride crystals that can be irritating if not broken down properly during the cooking process. So don't undercook the poi!

# Kalua Pork

*Kalua pork is the most traditional of all Hawaiian luau dishes. When we first heard of it, we actually thought that Kahlúa, the coffee-flavored liqueur, was somehow integrated into the recipe. How wrong we were. The term "kalua" is derived from the Hawaiian words* ka, *meaning "the," and* lua, *meaning "hole," referring to the underground hole, or* imu *(oven) the pork was cooked in. This dish is still made the traditional way, by cooking an entire pig in an underground oven, but our recipe is much easier. Digging a three-foot-deep pit in our backyards sounded like no fun at all to us—guess we're just lazy that way.  Note: Ti leaves are more traditional to Hawaiian cooking but can be difficult to find, so we use banana leaves in this recipe instead. Banana leaves are available at most Asian markets.*

Makes 8 servings

> 1 banana leaf
> 6 pounds boneless pork butt (shoulder), trimmed and cut into 6 chunks, about 2 inches thick
> 3 tablespoons Hawaiian sea salt or kosher salt
> 2 tablespoons Liquid Smoke flavoring
> 1 white onion, cut into ½-inch-thick rings
> 3 sprigs fresh rosemary
> 5 whole cloves garlic, peeled

Preheat the oven to 500°F. Lay a 9- by 11-inch piece of aluminum foil on the work surface. Place the banana leaf on top of the foil and arrange the pork on top. Sprinkle the pork all over with the salt and the Liquid Smoke. Arrange the onion rings, rosemary, and garlic on top of and around the pork. Fold the banana leaf up and over the pork to make a packet. Lay a second sheet of foil over the top, and seal the packet very tightly. Put the foil packet in a large roasting pan and fill it with 2 inches of water. Cover the roasting pan tightly with more foil, and steam the pork for 2 hours, until tender and an instant-read thermometer registers 160° F to 165° F. Let the pork rest wrapped for about 10 minutes. Unwrap the packet, shred the pork with a fork, and serve.

# Aloha Shrimp with Pineapple Fried Rice

*Pineapple can be used in both sweet and savory dishes, and this savory rice dish is a meal in itself. The rice is served from the fresh pineapple shell, making this a festive and fun dish perfect for a backyard luau.*

Makes 8 servings

1 large fresh pineapple
4 tablespoons peanut oil
4 cups cold cooked long grain rice
1 tablespoon grated fresh gingerroot
5 scallions, thinly sliced
3 cloves garlic, minced
1 cup shelled fresh peas (or frozen)
1½ pounds medium-size shrimp (61 to 75 shrimp), peeled and deveined
1 teaspoon salt
½ teaspoon freshly ground black pepper

Slice the pineapple in half lengthwise and hollow out each half, removing the pineapple meat and discarding the tough center core. Cut the pineapple into ½-inch cubes. Reserve 1 cup of cubed pineapple, saving the rest for another use.

In a wok or heavy skillet, heat the oil over medium-high heat until it is hot but not smoking. Add the rice and stir-fry for about 15 minutes, or until the rice is slightly browned. Lower the heat to medium and add the ginger, scallions, garlic, peas, and the reserved pineapple to the rice and stir-fry another 3 to 4 minutes, mixing well to combine. Add the shrimp and stir-fry until just cooked through, about 4 minutes.

Immediately turn the rice mixture out into a large bowl so that the shrimp do not overcook. Season with salt and pepper. Keep warm.

When ready to serve, place the pineapple halves cut side down under the broiler for 5 minutes or until heated through. Spoon the warm rice into the pineapple halves and serve.

*One of the very nicest things about life is the way we must regularly stop whatever it is we are doing and devote our attention to eating.*
—Luciano Pavarotti

## Tips for a Successful
# Hawaiian-Inspired Dinner

- Arrange bamboo torches throughout the backyard. Don't forget to line some up along your entryway for your guests to follow to the door.

- Use raffia table skirts to decorate the serving table or dining area.

- Encourage guests to wear their best luau attire. Give a prize for the most original ideas.

- Plastic leis can be bought at any party store. For a special party gift for your guests, order fresh, fragrant leis from a florist. Or present each guest with a beautiful flower as he or she arrives. They can wear them behind their ear or in a buttonhole.

- Fresh pineapples and other tropical fruit surrounded by fresh flowers makes a perfect centerpiece.

- To set the mood, have Hawaiian music playing in the background. You can't go wrong with Don Ho.

- Hire Hawaiian dancers through your local community college, or hire teachers from a local dance studio, to perform and teach your guests to hula.

- Hollow out fresh pineapples for your guests to use as cups, or purchase plastic pineapple cups from a party store.

- Elvis impersonator, anyone? Hiring an Elvis impersonator, if only long enough for him to sing "Blue Hawaii," is great fun.

# Macadamia Nut Pie with Creamy Coconut Ice Cream

*Macadamia nuts are a common feature of Hawaiian cuisine, and nearly every gift shop on the islands sells boxes of chocolate-covered macadamias. This recipe is a spin on southern pecan pie, with an island twist. Even though he doesn't particularly like nuts, Michelle's son Collin loves this pie; when she bakes one, he can't wait to dig right in. You can serve the pie warm, but it tastes better straight from the fridge with a scoop of Creamy Coconut Ice Cream on the side.*

Makes 1 pie or enough for 8 servings

1½ cups all-purpose flour
2 teaspoons sugar
½ teaspoon salt
6 tablespoons unsalted butter, chilled, cut into ½-inch pieces
2 tablespoons solid vegetable shortening, chilled, cut into ½-inch pieces
4 tablespoons ice water, plus more if needed

1½ cups roasted unsalted macadamia nuts
⅔ cup packed light brown sugar
3 large eggs
½ cup dark corn syrup
½ stick (4 tablespoons) unsalted butter, melted
3 teaspoons pure vanilla extract

Creamy Coconut Ice Cream (recipe follows)

To prepare the pie crust, pulse the flour, sugar, and salt in the bowl of a food processor fitted with a steel blade. Add the butter and shortening in 2 or 3 additions until the mixture resembles coarse meal. Slowly add the water and pulse until the dough starts to form clumps. If the dough seems too dry, add water by the teaspoonful until the dough reaches the desired consistency.

Turn the dough out onto a lightly floured work surface. Gather the dough together, shaping it into a ball, then flatten the dough into a disk about ½-inch thick. Wrap the dough in plastic wrap and refrigerate for at least an hour.

Preheat the oven to 325°F.

When you are ready to assemble the pie, allow the dough to soften slightly at room temperature. Flour the work surface and the rolling pin, and roll the dough out into an 11-inch disk, about ⅛-inch thick. Transfer the dough to a 9-inch pie pan, build the dough up around the rim about ¾ inch; using your fingertips, crimp the edges to form a decorative border.

To make the pie filling, put the roasted nuts in a heavy-duty plastic sandwich bag and, using a hammer or rolling pin, break the macadamia nuts into small, bite-size pieces. Set aside.

In a large bowl, whisk together the sugar, eggs, corn syrup, butter, and vanilla until well combined. Cover the bottom of the prepared unbaked pie crust evenly with the nuts, then pour the sugar mixture over them, smoothing the mixture with the back of a spoon.

Bake the pie on the middle oven rack until the center puffs slightly, about 50 minutes. If the center is still wobbly, bake for 5 minutes more, or until the custard is completely cooked in the middle. To serve warm, cool 10 minutes on a wire rack, or serve chilled.

## Creamy Coconut Ice Cream

Makes 1 quart or enough for 8 servings

> One 13.5-ounce can (1¾ cups) unsweetened coconut milk
> 1 cup heavy cream
> 1 cup half-and-half
> ¼ teaspoon salt
> ¼ cup coconut-flavored rum
> 8 egg yolks
> 1 cup sugar

Put the coconut milk, cream, half-and-half, and salt in a medium-size saucepan set over medium heat. While stirring, allow the mixture to barely come to a boil, then remove the pan from the heat. Add the rum, cover, and set aside.

Put the egg yolks in a medium-size bowl and whisk until thoroughly blended. Slowly add the sugar to the egg yolks, and whisk until all the sugar is combined.

While whisking, add the milk mixture a small amount at a time to the egg mixture in order to temper the eggs and prevent them from curdling. When about one third of the milk mixture has been added to the eggs, still whisking, pour the remaining milk mixture into the eggs.

Pour the milk and egg mixture back into the saucepan and set it over medium-low heat. Whisking constantly, cook the custard until it reaches 170°F on an instant-read thermometer, or until the mixture thickens slightly and coats the back of a spoon.

Pour the custard through a fine-mesh sieve placed over a large bowl. Cover the bowl and allow the custard to sit at room temperature for 15 minutes, then let the custard chill in the refrigerator for at least 4 hours or, preferably, overnight. Pour the custard into the ice cream maker and process according to the manufacturer's instructions. Serve the ice cream right away or, for a firmer texture, let it chill for 2 hours in the freezer.

# Atco Gourmet Dinner Club

If you are lucky enough to be an invited dinner guest at the Atco Gourmet Dinner Club, you just might be handed a tambourine and asked to join in a spontaneous jam session. This musical bunch all call Atco, New Jersey, home, and when they are not enjoying each other's company around the table, some of them perform together in a local band.

Annette Rinker and her husband, Rich, had attended the Atco Gourmet Dinner Club as guests, but it wasn't until November 2000 that there was an opening and they were asked to become permanent members. This was music to Annette's ears, as she had known about the club since its inception in 1998. Annette's friends Sally and Bob Browne founded the Atco Gourmet Dinner Club with the idea of combining two of their favorite things: food and friends. "I don't think Sally and Bob have ever missed one of our dinners!" said Annette.

The club consists of four permanent couples, but one or more guest couples are usually asked to join in the fun. "The guest couples add a new element to our group and keep us on our toes," said Annette. "The group gets together about every six to eight weeks. We wish it were more often, but we all have such busy lives."

Cooking club co-founder Bob Browne manages a website for the group that includes photographs, descriptions of past club dinners, and any upcoming news about the group. "The website is a great way for all of us to keep informed and to catalogue our recipes from past events," said Annette. Members decide on the theme for the next dinner during the current get-together and then visit the website to see the course rotation list where each member is assigned to bring either a soup, side dish, salad, or appetizer. The host couple makes the main course, and the invited guest couples bring dessert. Each cook brings the recipe of their prepared dish to the dinner and it is posted on the website. "Each of us really goes all-out when it is our turn to host," said Annette. "We all enjoy good food, and one of our members, Jim Wert, has even gone to cooking school. We call Jim the 'Soup Nazi' [from the TV show *Seinfeld*] because he makes some of the most delicious soups. Jim actually met his namesake at an Atlantic City gourmet food show and now has a signed photo from him," said Annette.

While this group is serious about food, having fun and just being together are what's most important to them. "When we get together, I know it's going to be a fun night," said Annette. "I get a delicious meal, conversation with good friends, and I only have to cook one dish." Since this group has been getting together for so long, they have many years of memorable cooking club events behind them. Highlights include: a night devoted to comfort food, an all-American gourmet barbecue with all the trimmings, an Asian-themed night, and a night where they "kicked it up a notch" and did a tribute to Emeril Lagasse. For the comfort-food theme, Rinker asked everyone to come in their sweats or pajamas. "I made individual chicken pot pies for every guest that night. We had two guest couples that were going to be joining us as well, so that was a lot of ramekins I was going to need," said Annette. "Luckily, I just so happened to find all of them at the dollar store. The price was right, and the pot pies turned out amazing!"

This group doesn't just eat together—they play music together too. In 2003, Annette and club co-founder Bob Browne formed the band Backyard and in 2005 brought Annette's husband, Rich, into the group. "Our style is a little bit rock, a little bit blues, and a little bit folk," said Annette. "We like to support our local music scene here in Atco and play at different venues throughout town." Rich plays percussion, Bob plays acoustic guitar and does backup vocals, and Annette sings lead vocals. "You never know when we may just start playing music together while at a cooking club event," said Annette. "Rich will start playing his Djembe [an African drum], I'll start singing, and the next thing you know, tambourines are passed around for those who want to join in!"

Channeling their creativity into food and music, it's no wonder this group has been around for as long as it has. We think ten years of creating wonderful meals together is only just the beginning.

# One Night in Bangkok:
## Thai Cuisine

*You Are Cordially Invited to Enjoy One Night in Bangkok*
*As We Experience an Evening of Thai Cuisine*
*Where Every Dish Has a Distinctive Blend of Flavor,*
*Color, and Texture*

## Menu

Mango and Lemongrass Cocktail

Pork Satay with Peanut Sauce

Steamed Clams and Mussels in Thai Green Curry Broth

Roasted Green Bean Salad with Chilies, Garlic, and Ginger

Hot and Sour Shrimp Soup with Rice Noodles

Sesame and Lime Jasmine Rice

Thai Red Curry Beef

Coconut Tapioca with Minty Lemongrass-Ginger Syrup and Mangoes

# Mango and Lemongrass Cocktail

*Entertaining with friends and family is a big part of our lives, and being a part of a cooking club has given us the ability to entertain with confidence . . . even in extreme situations. Every summer, Dina's sister Lamia, Lamia's two sons, their cousin Odette, and Odette's four kids come and visit Dina for a week. Her house turns into mass chaos, but it is one of Dina's favorite times of the year because the three women laugh, talk, and cook up a storm together. Dina was in the process of writing this book during one of their visits and she whipped up this fruity Thai-inspired drink that is cool and refreshing on a hot day.*

Makes 8 cocktails

> 4 medium-size mangoes, peeled, pitted, and roughly chopped (about 4 cups)
> 2 cups Lemongrass Syrup (recipe follows)
> 1 cup vodka
> 1 cup ice
> 8 fresh mint sprigs for garnish

Purée the mangoes in a blender with ¼ cup of the lemongrass syrup. Add the remaining syrup, vodka, and ice, and blend until smooth. Strain into 8 chilled 8-ounce glasses and garnish with mint sprigs.

## Lemongrass Syrup

Makes 2 cups or enough for 8 cocktails

> 2 stalks fresh lemongrass
> 2 cups water
> 1 cup sugar
> 20 large fresh mint leaves

Trim the root ends of the lemongrass stalks, and remove and discard the tough outer layers. Bruise the stalks with the back of a chef's knife, and coarsely chop the stalks.

Combine the water, sugar, lemongrass, and mint in a medium-size saucepan. Bring the mixture to a boil, then simmer over low heat for 10 minutes. Remove the pan from the heat, cover, and set it aside for 20 minutes to infuse. Strain the syrup into a medium-size bowl, cover, and let it cool in the refrigerator for up to 5 days.

*Food is so primal, so essential a part of our lives, often the mere sharing of recipes with strangers turns them into good friends.*
—Jasmine Heiler

## Tips for a Successful
# Thai-Inspired Dinner

- Give lemongrass plants to your guests for party favors.

- At each place setting, arrange some bamboo stalks in stoneware bowls packed with gravel.

- For a centerpiece, float orchids in inexpensive rice bowls for an eye-level arrangement, and use potted orchids to add height.

- Give your centerpiece an exotic look by using orchids, bamboo, bear grass, large lilies, and curly willow.

- Use silks of different colors and textures for table runners.

- Burning subtle sandalwood incense creates a mood instantly.

- Do as many Thai families do and dine seated on the floor. Have plenty of cushy pillows for your guests to sit on, and arrange the food on a low table or coffee table.

# Pork Satay with Peanut Sauce

*Every year, we host a Halloween party with our dear friend Susanne Nielsen. For Susanne, this party is all about the hilarious costumes, good friends, and these really great jello shots that she makes every year. For us, well, it's about all those things too, but it's also all about the food. We always try to come up with dishes that go with the Halloween theme, and one year, Dina made these pork satay appetizers look like witches' fingers. They flew off the table so fast, we're not sure if anyone even noticed her creative design attempts. But for any time of year, these grilled appetizers are always a hit. Note: For this recipe, you will need 16 bamboo skewers.*

Makes 8 appetizer servings

1 pork tenderloin (about ¾ pound), cut into 3- by 1- by ¼-inch-thick strips

1 stalk fresh lemongrass, tough outer layers and green parts removed, minced (about ¼ cup)

2 fresh Thai red chili peppers, seeded and minced (about ½ tablespoon)

¼ cup canned unsweetened coconut milk

1 shallot, minced

½ tablespoon soy sauce

1 tablespoon *nam pla* (Thai fish sauce)

2 cloves garlic, minced

½ tablespoon brown sugar

½ teaspoon ground coriander

½ teaspoon ground cumin

½ teaspoon salt

¼ teaspoon freshly ground black pepper

¼ teaspoon ground ginger

Peanut Sauce (recipe follows)

Place the pork strips in a shallow baking dish. Combine the lemongrass, chili peppers, coconut milk, shallot, soy sauce, fish sauce, garlic, brown sugar, coriander, cumin, salt, pepper, and ginger and mix well. Pour the mixture over the pork, turn to coat, cover, and let the pork marinate in the refrigerator for at least 4 and up to 24 hours.

Soak the skewers in water for 1 hour.

Preheat an outdoor grill or use a grill pan on the stove set over medium-high heat. Thread 3 to 4 pieces of the pork onto each skewer, weaving the skewer in and out of the strip of pork so that it stays in place while grilling. Brush the grill lightly with vegetable oil. Grill the pork for 2 or 3 minutes on each side, until nicely seared and cooked through. Transfer the pork to a platter and serve immediately, along with the Peanut Sauce.

## Peanut Sauce

Makes 1¼ cups or enough for 8 servings

¾ cup canned unsweetened coconut milk

1 teaspoon red curry paste (such as Thai Kitchen), or to taste

½ cup smooth peanut butter

1 tablespoon tamarind concentrate or paste, or ⅓ cup freshly squeezed lime juice

1 teaspoon *nam pla* (Thai fish sauce)

1 tablespoon chopped fresh cilantro

1 tablespoon chopped roasted peanuts

Pour the coconut milk in a small saucepan and set over medium heat for 2 minutes. Whisk in the curry paste and cook for 1 minute until the paste is completely incorporated into the milk. Whisk in the peanut butter, tamarind, and fish sauce and cook for 1 minute. If it becomes too thick, thin the sauce with a few teaspoons of water. Pour the sauce into a serving bowl and garnish with the cilantro and peanuts.

# Steamed Clams and Mussels in Thai Green Curry Broth

*One of the things we love about entertaining is sharing good food with great friends and creating special memories that last a lifetime. We have these really good friends, Tom and Sue Jas, and our families spend a lot of time together. Tom's birthday and Dina's husband Roland's birthday are six days apart, and we get together for a big birthday bash every year. When Dina heard Tom loved Thai food, she created this dish for his birthday dinner. He made her day when she saw him dunking a bowl into the remaining broth left at the bottom of the pot and drinking it before he thought anyone could see. You may need to search a bit to find the kaffir lime leaves, but try to get them; they make a big difference. A loaf of fresh, crusty bread would be great to sop up the sauce, too, or to make this a full meal, serve over a bed of steamed white rice.*

Makes 8 appetizer servings

2 pounds littleneck clams, scrubbed

2 pounds mussels, scrubbed and debearded

2 stalks fresh lemongrass

¼ cup unsalted butter

2 shallots, thinly sliced

6 cloves garlic, minced

2 tablespoons minced fresh gingerroot

2 teaspoons green curry paste (such as Thai Kitchen), or to taste

6 kaffir lime leaves, or 1 tablespoon lime zest

Two 13.5-ounce cans unsweetened coconut milk

1 cup dry white wine, like Chardonnay

¼ cup freshly squeezed lime juice (about two limes)

1 tablespoon *nam pla* (Thai fish sauce)

½ teaspoon salt

¼ teaspoon freshly ground black pepper

⅓ cup slivered fresh Thai or regular basil leaves

Discard any clams or mussels that aren't tightly closed and that remain open when you tap one against another.

Trim the root ends of the lemongrass stalks, and remove and discard the tough outer layers. Bruise the stalks with the back of a chef's knife, and coarsely chop the stalks.

Melt the butter in a large pot over medium-high heat. Add the shallots and sauté until soft and translucent, about 2 minutes. Add the garlic and ginger and sauté for 1 minute. Add the curry paste and stir until shallot mixture is coated with the paste. Stir in the lemongrass, kaffir lime leaves, coconut milk, and wine. Bring the mixture to a simmer and cook over low heat for 20 minutes. Remove the lemongrass and lime leaves, and add the lime juice, fish sauce, salt, and pepper. Add the clams and mussels, cover the pot, and cook for 8 minutes. Discard any clams or mussels with shells that remain closed after cooking. Add the basil. Replace the lid and gently shake the pot.

Pour the clams, mussels, and sauce into a warm serving bowl and serve.

# Roasted Green Bean Salad with Chilies, Garlic, and Ginger

*One of our cooking club members, Lisa Frazzetta, loves her food fresh from the market. She has often joked that the grocers know her by name since she is in there so often, and if you were to look in her freezer, it would be practically empty since she doesn't even like to freeze leftovers. Her preference for fresh seasonal produce inspired this green bean salad that gets tossed with plenty of fresh herbs. If fresh green beans aren't in season, feel free to use frozen—we won't tell Lisa.*

Makes 8 servings

> 2 tablespoons peanut oil
> 2 Thai red chili peppers, seeded, cut into fine slices
> 6 cloves garlic, minced
> 2 tablespoons grated fresh gingerroot
> 1 teaspoon salt
> 2 pounds fresh or frozen green beans (thawed, if frozen), trimmed
> 2 tablespoons *nam pla* (Thai fish sauce)

Juice of 2 limes (about 4 tablespoons)

2 tablespoons sugar

½ cup torn fresh mint leaves

½ cup torn fresh basil leaves (preferably Thai basil)

½ cup coarsely chopped dry-roasted peanuts

Preheat the oven to 450°F.

Whisk together the oil, chili peppers, garlic, ginger, and salt in a large bowl. Add the green beans and toss. Transfer the beans to 2 baking sheets, spreading them in a single layer on each sheet. Roast the beans until tender, about 10 minutes.

While the beans are cooking, combine the fish sauce, lime juice, and sugar in a small bowl and whisk until the sugar is dissolved.

Remove the beans from the oven and toss them in a large bowl with the fish sauce mixture, mint, and basil. Garnish the salad with the peanuts and serve immediately.

# Hot and Sour Shrimp Soup with Rice Noodles

*There are five ingredients we usually associate with Thai cuisine: lemongrass, kaffir lime leaves, tamarind paste, fish sauce, and galangal. This recipe uses all five. If you can, make every effort to find them before making this soup. The beauty of Thai food is that it is complex and fragrant, hot and sweet, all at once. You'll miss the essence of this dish with too many substitutions, but if you must, you can use gingerroot for galangal, or lime zest for kaffir lime leaves. If you can't find the tamarind, use the juice of two limes instead of just one.*

Makes 8 servings

6 ounces dried rice stick noodles

4 stalks fresh lemongrass

2 tablespoons vegetable oil

6 cloves garlic, cut into thin slices

4 shallots, cut into thin slices

One 1-inch piece fresh galangal or gingerroot, cut into thin slices

6 kaffir lime leaves, roughly chopped, or 4 teaspoons lime zest

2 Thai red chili peppers with seeds, cut into thin slices

1 teaspoon salt

2 pounds (80 to 100) medium-size shrimp, peeled, shells reserved

2 quarts chicken stock

2 cups sliced button mushrooms

2 cups chopped baby bok choy

¼ cup *nam pla* (Thai fish sauce)

¼ cup tamarind concentrate or paste

Juice of 1 lime (about 2 tablespoons)

3 teaspoons sugar

½ cup chopped fresh cilantro

½ cup chopped fresh Thai or regular basil

Bring a medium saucepan of water to a boil. Add the noodles and stir; remove the pan from the heat. Let stand until the noodles soften, 7 to 10 minutes; drain and set aside.

Trim the root ends of the lemongrass stalks, and remove and discard the tough outer layers. Cut the stalks into 3-inch pieces and bruise them with the back of a chef's knife.

Heat the oil in a large pot over medium-high heat. Add the lemongrass, garlic, shallots, galangal, kaffir lime leaves, chili peppers, salt, and shrimp shells, and cook for 4 minutes, stirring frequently. Add the stock, turn the heat to high, and bring to a boil. Lower the heat and simmer for 20 minutes, skimming off any foam, if necessary.

Strain the broth, return it to the pot, and bring it to a gentle simmer over medium heat. Add the mushrooms and bok choy and cook for 2 minutes. Add the fish sauce, tamarind, lime juice, sugar, and shrimp, and cook for another 2 minutes.

Divide the noodles among 8 soup bowls. Add the cilantro and basil to the soup. Ladle the soup over the noodles and serve.

# Sesame and Lime Jasmine Rice

*One of the most important things we have learned from being in a cooking club is how to plan a menu. The first time Dina hosted a cooking club dinner, she decided to do a Thai-themed menu. Thai food can be very spicy, and it's important to balance each dish with the right mix of flavors. Simple steamed rice is usually all you need to complement a curry, but she found that the citrusy lime zest and the nutty sesame seeds in this rice dish are a perfect foil for the spicy Thai Red Curry Beef on page 141.*

Makes 8 servings

2 tablespoons unsalted butter
1 tablespoon sesame oil
2 cups jasmine rice
3 cups water
1½ teaspoons salt
2 tablespoons sesame seeds, toasted
Zest from 3 limes

Combine the butter and sesame oil in a large saucepan over moderate heat until the butter has melted. Add the rice and cook, stirring, for 3 to 5 minutes, until lightly browned. Stir in the water and salt, bring to a boil, reduce the heat to low, and cook, covered, for 15 minutes until all the water is absorbed. Remove the rice from the heat and let sit, still covered, for 5 minutes. Fluff the rice with a fork and stir in the sesame seeds and lime zest. Serve immediately.

# Thai Red Curry Beef

*Dina makes this dish every time her brother Sam comes to visit. He loves Thai food, and this recipe is so easy to make. Most of the ingredients are usually in our pantries, so we can make it at the last minute and have it ready on the table in no time. We often make this curry with chicken, but you can use any protein you like, including shrimp or tofu. Thai curry pastes vary in strength and spiciness from brand to brand. Recipes ask for anything from 1 teaspoon to an entire jar in a dish that serves 4. Be sure to taste as you go along, and add more curry if you prefer a spicier dish.*

Makes 8 servings

2 tablespoons olive oil

4 shallots, thinly sliced

1 to 2 tablespoons Thai red curry paste (such as Thai Kitchen), or to taste

¼ cup tomato paste

Two 13.5-ounce cans unsweetened coconut milk

2 cups low-sodium chicken broth

Two 15-ounce cans straw mushrooms, drained

6 kaffir lime leaves, or 4 teaspoons lime zest

2 pounds top sirloin or other tender cut, cut into strips 2- by 1- by ¼-inch thick

4 tablespoons *nam pla* (Thai fish sauce)

2 tablespoons palm sugar or brown sugar

2 large tomatoes, diced

2 pounds asparagus, tough stem ends snapped off, cut into 1-inch pieces

½ cup slivered fresh Thai or regular basil leaves

In a large, wide pot, heat the oil over medium-high heat. Add the shallots, curry paste, and tomato paste, and stir until fragrant, about 3 minutes. Add the coconut milk, chicken broth, mushrooms, and kaffir lime leaves or zest. Cook, uncovered, until the sauce has slightly reduced and thickened, about 25 minutes. Stir in the beef, fish sauce, and sugar and cook for 3 minutes. Add the tomatoes and asparagus and cook for 5 minutes more, until the asparagus is tender. Sprinkle with basil and serve with the Sesame and Lime Jasmine Rice on page 140.

# Coconut Tapioca with Minty Lemongrass-Ginger Syrup and Mangoes

*During a cooking club gathering, one of our members, Carolyn, prepared a coconut rice pudding with mangoes that was so delicious we still talk about it nearly six years later. Here is a version of that pudding prepared with tapioca, although you can substitute rice if you prefer. This dessert makes for a great presentation, too.*

Makes 8 servings

 3 cups whole milk
 One 13.5-ounce can unsweetened coconut milk
 ⅔ cup small-pearl tapioca
 3 tablespoons sugar
 Lemongrass-Ginger Syrup (recipe follows)
 2 large ripe mangoes, peeled and cut into ¼-inch dice (about 2 cups)
 ¼ cup toasted sweetened coconut
 8 sprigs fresh mint

Whisk together the milk, coconut milk, tapioca, and sugar in a heavy saucepan and cook over medium heat until the mixture comes to a boil. Reduce the heat to low. Stirring frequently, let the pudding simmer, uncovered, for 25 minutes or until thickened and coats the back of a spoon, being careful that the pudding does not scorch. Transfer the pudding to a large bowl and wrap with plastic wrap, smoothing the wrap directly on the surface of the pudding so that a skin does not form. Chill the pudding in the refrigerator for at least 30 minutes before serving.

Divide the pudding among 8 dessert bowls. Drizzle 2 tablespoons of Lemongrass Syrup over each serving and garnish with the mango, coconut, and a sprig of mint.

# Lemongrass-Ginger Syrup

Makes 1 cup or enough for 8 servings

> 1 stalk fresh lemongrass
>
> ¾ cup water
>
> ¾ cup sugar
>
> ½-inch piece fresh gingerroot, peeled and thinly sliced
>
> 20 fresh mint leaves

Trim the root ends of the lemongrass stalk, and remove and discard the tough outer layer. Bruise the stalk with the back of a chef's knife, and coarsely chop the stalk.

Combine the water, sugar, lemongrass, ginger, and mint in a medium-size saucepan over medium-high heat. Bring the syrup to a boil, stirring until the sugar is dissolved. Reduce the heat to low and let simmer for 10 minutes. Remove the pan from the heat, cover, and set it aside for 20 minutes to infuse. Strain the syrup through a fine sieve into a medium-size bowl, cover, and let it chill in the refrigerator for up to 5 days.

Jon Emanuel of Denver, Colorado, is the kind of guy you know you are going to like even before you meet him. He reminds us of Duff Goldman from the Food Network program "Ace of Cakes," and he is an accomplished chef himself. About wanting to start his own cooking club, Emanuel says, "I figured the best way to find people who actually had a clue about food was to seek out people who had been around the block in terms of cuisine, travel, and culture. I wanted to find people who enjoy going beyond the typical foods they are used to."

Thanks to the Internet, there are countless ways for like-minded people to come together and find each other. For Emanuel, all it took was a posting on the social networking Web site Meetup.com. Meetup.com claims it is the world's largest community of local gatherings of clubs and groups, and in a typical month, more than 74,000 groups will "meet up" from around the world. Emanuel was looking specifically for adventurous eaters to form a club with him. Thus, the Denver Adventurous Eaters Club was born. That adventurous spirit comes naturally to Emanuel, who worked at a wilderness lodge in Alaska for six years as an executive chef, and has made seven deployments to the South Pole working as either a sous chef or as an executive chef.

The Denver Adventurous Eaters Club, or DAEC, has been eating adventurously since 2007. They have more than two hundred members who are affiliated through the club's Web site, but a typical gathering will have anywhere from ten to forty members in attendance. Most of the members are professional men and women in their twenties, thirties, and forties who want to meet new people with common interests. Some are chefs, and all like to eat on the culinary "edge."

What do we mean by "the edge"? How about braised pig hearts, fried lamb kidneys, coagulated pork blood mixed with intestines and pickles, lamb hearts, homemade headcheese, duck-tongue stomach soup, frog porridge, and pigs' eyes, for starters.

Any cooking club that cooks intestines and eyeballs is no ordinary club. Aside from eating foods that some would consider unusual or, well, "challenging," this group has a good sense of humor, as well. At a meeting where the DAEC got together to cook and taste different parts of two "heritage" hogs, they called the gathering, "Praise the Lard! A Pig-Part Extravaganza." At another favorite gathering at a local park, the club roasted a whole goat and served it to more than forty people. That meeting was billed as "Hey Kids, Get Yer Goat On!"

As the group becomes even more popular, securing a venue with enough space to get together can be a challenge. Luckily, Emanuel is a resourceful guy who has held meetings at a local Denver park or a favorite restaurant. He has also hosted meetings at his workplace. Emanuel is the executive chef at Project Angel Heart, a nonprofit organization whose mission is "to promote the health, dignity, and self-sufficiency of people living with HIV/AIDS, cancer, and other life-threatening illnesses by providing nutritious home-delivered meals with care and compassion."

For Emanuel, hosting gatherings in the Angel Heart industrial kitchen is a great way to accommodate lots of people in one place. For each DAEC gathering, Emanuel is usually in charge of the main dish, and the guests who attend bring side dishes they've prepared at home to accompany the entrée. Emanuel also asks each member to bring money to cover his costs, with any extra being donated to Project Angel Heart. "The participants are always enthusiastic about the eating and the giving," says Emanuel. Emanuel does a majority of the prep work for the main course, but he asks members to lend a hand when it's needed.

When asked what he enjoys most about the group, Emanuel says, "I like being surprised. I get surprised by the foods, surprised by who the members are, and by who tries what. At one event we had four eyeballs to taste, and the two women who jumped up to try them were the last people I would have expected to try something like that. It was a pretty cool moment."

The guidelines of the group are written with Emanuel's typical tongue-in-cheek style. He says you might want to think twice about joining the group "if you are strictly the meat-and-potatoes type, if you like your steak well done, if you only eat white meat, if you are a vegetarian, and if Taco Bell is too spicy for you." Basically, says Emanuel, "if you wouldn't think of trying roast duck chins or tempura fish heads, or anything not available at Cracker Barrel, this is not the group for you."

When asked for one word to describe his group he says, "Willing. Willing to try new things, willing to cook, willing to contribute money, and sweat." He says he "just wants to spread the love—and the marrow on toast." Praise the lard indeed!

# Autumn Leaves:
## Celebrating the Autumnal Equinox

*The Air Is Starting to Cool, and the Leaves Are Changing Color*
*Come in from the Cold and Enjoy the Tastes and*
*Smells of an Autumn Harvest Feast*

### Menu

Pomegranate Margarita

Mushroom and Goat Cheese Crostini

Roasted Pumpkin Soup with Mascarpone Maple Cream
and Spiced Pumpkin Seeds

Harvest Salad with Apples, Pecans, Dried Cherries, and Blue Cheese

Port-Braised Lamb Shanks

Fontina and Thyme Polenta

Roasted Brussels Sprouts with Pancetta and Shallots

Gingerbread Cupcakes with Lemon Cream and Candied Pistachio Sprinkles

# Pomegranate Margarita

*Some of our favorite cooking club moments take place during the "cocktail hour," when we all first arrive and catch up on what's been happening since we last met a month earlier. It is a truly sensory experience: everyone's laughing and talking, glasses are clinking, alcohol is flowing, and the drinks are sweet. This easy recipe for Pomegranate Margaritas is a great way to kick off your dinner party.*

Makes 8 margaritas

>  2 cups pomegranate juice
>  1 cup gold tequila
>  ½ cup Triple Sec or any orange-flavored liqueur
>  ½ cup freshly squeezed lime juice (about 4 limes)
>  Pomegranate seeds (optional)

Pour the pomegranate juice, tequila, Triple Sec, and lime juice into a pitcher and stir to combine. Fill 8 margarita glasses with ice cubes and divide the margarita mixture evenly among the glasses. Garnish with pomegranate seeds.


# Mushroom and Goat Cheese Crostini

*One of Dina's first jobs was at the CBS affiliate television station in Fresno, California. A few of her friends and co-workers there formed a cooking club, which she remembers fondly. It was her very first cooking club, as it was for all of them, and they truly had no idea what they were doing. They didn't know a shallot from a leek, or what they were supposed to do with a mortar and pestle, and they really had no business in a kitchen equipped with gas and flames. Dina was recently talking with Jennifer Whitney, a friend and former member of that club, and they reminisced about those days, trying to remember some of their themes or menus. But all they could remember were the laughs, the really good times, and that they made an awful lot of recipes with goat cheese. Dina hasn't changed much, because she still uses goat cheese every chance she gets, and this is one of her favorites.*

Makes 18 crostini or enough for 8 servings

>  3 tablespoons unsalted butter
>  4 cloves garlic, minced

1 pound mixed mushrooms, such as cremini, button, shiitake, and oyster, cut into thin slices

1 teaspoon minced fresh thyme

½ cup dry sherry

2 tablespoons freshly squeezed lemon juice (about ⅔ lemon)

¼ teaspoon salt

¼ teaspoon freshly ground black pepper

18 thin slices sourdough baguette

4 ounces fresh goat cheese, softened at room temperature

¼ cup chopped parsley

Preheat the broiler.

Melt the butter in a large skillet over medium heat. Add the garlic and cook for 1 minute. Raise the heat to medium-high and add the mushrooms. Sauté until brown and caramelized, about 10 minutes. Add the thyme and cook for 1 minute, then add the sherry. Cook until the skillet is almost dry, 1 to 2 minutes. Stir in the lemon juice and season with salt and pepper to taste. Keep warm.

Place the baguette slices on a sheet pan and toast them under the preheated broiler until crispy, about 3 to 5 minutes for each side. Once toasted, spread them evenly with the goat cheese and top with the mushroom mixture. Sprinkle the crostini with parsley and serve.

# Roasted Pumpkin Soup with Mascarpone Maple Cream and Spiced Pumpkin Seeds

*Our cooking club often takes cooking classes together, and during one of those classes, the chef prepared a butternut squash soup that fellow cooking club member Lisa Frazzetta described as "epic," and we couldn't agree more. We have been putting squash soups on our cooking club menu consistently since that class, and this version using pumpkin is one of our favorites. Look for sugar pumpkins instead of the larger jack-o'-lanterns—they are sweeter and less stringy. You can use any kind of winter squash you like, such as butternut or acorn squash.*

Makes 8 servings

> 2 small cooking pumpkins, about 2 pounds each
> ½ stick (4 tablespoons) unsalted butter
> 2 medium leeks, white parts only, chopped
> 2 medium russet potatoes, peeled and diced
> 6 cups low-sodium chicken stock
> 1 teaspoon salt
> ¼ teaspoon freshly ground black pepper
> Mascarpone Maple Cream (recipe follows)
> Spiced Pumpkin Seeds (recipe follows)

To prepare the soup, preheat the oven to 375°F. Cut the pumpkins in half and scoop out the seeds and strings. Place the pumpkins, cut side down, on an oiled baking sheet. Roast in the oven until tender, about 45 to 60 minutes. Cool for 20 minutes, then scoop the pulp into a large bowl and set aside. Discard the pumpkin skin.

Melt the butter in a large saucepan over medium-high heat. Add the leeks and cook until softened, about 5 minutes. Add the potatoes, chicken stock, and pumpkin and bring to a boil. Reduce the heat and simmer for 30 to 40 minutes or until the potatoes are tender.

Working in batches, pour the soup into a blender jar and purée it until smooth. It will take several batches to purée all the soup. Be careful with the hot soup, and do not overfill the blender jar. Strain the soup through a sieve back into the saucepan and season it with salt and pepper.

To serve, ladle the soup into bowls, drizzle with the mascarpone maple cream, and sprinkle with the spiced pumpkin seeds.

## Mascarpone Maple Cream
Makes ½ cup or enough for 8 servings

>  4 tablespoons mascarpone cheese
>  2 tablespoons heavy cream
>  3 tablespoons pure maple syrup

Combine the mascarpone and heavy cream in a small bowl, mixing until it becomes creamy. Stir in the maple syrup, cover the bowl, and refrigerate until ready to use.

## Spiced Pumpkin Seeds
Makes ½ cup or enough for 8 servings

>  1 tablespoon sugar
>  2 teaspoons garlic powder
>  2 teaspoons onion powder
>  1 teaspoon salt
>  ½ teaspoon curry powder
>  ½ teaspoon dried thyme
>  ⅛ teaspoon cayenne pepper
>  ⅓ cup hulled pumpkin seeds (also called *pepitas*)
>  1 tablespoon unsalted butter, melted

Preheat the oven to 250°F. Combine the sugar, garlic powder, onion powder, salt, curry powder, thyme, and cayenne in a small bowl. In a medium-size bowl, toss the pumpkin seeds and the melted butter with the spice mixture. Transfer the seeds to a baking sheet, spreading them out in a single layer, and roast for 30 minutes, stirring the seeds every 10 minutes, until the seeds are lightly browned and crunchy. Once the seeds cool, they can be stored in an airtight container for up to 1 week at room temperature, or refrigerated for up to 1 month.

# Harvest Salad with Apples, Pecans, Dried Cherries, and Blue Cheese

*Dina's best friend from high school, Jennifer Post, recently moved to Sacramento after having lived in San Francisco, where she was surrounded by some of the best cuisine in the world. One of the first things they did after her move was visit a farmer's market where they found the makings for this salad, which uses very simple ingredients to make a spectacular combination.*

Makes 8 servings

3 tablespoons white wine vinegar
1 tablespoon Dijon mustard
2 small cloves garlic, minced
2 teaspoons honey
½ teaspoon salt
¼ teaspoon freshly ground black pepper
⅓ cup extra-virgin olive oil

1 cup dried cherries
½ cup hot water
10 ounces mixed baby greens
2 medium Granny Smith apples, or another variety of tart apple such as Gravenstein or pippin, peeled and cut into ⅛-inch-thick slices
4 ounces blue cheese
½ cup chopped toasted pecans

To make the dressing, whisk together the vinegar, mustard, garlic, honey, salt, and pepper. Slowly whisk in the oil. The vinaigrette may be made 1 day ahead and chilled, covered.

To make the salad, put the cherries in a small bowl with the hot water. Let the cherries sit for 10 minutes until they plump up. Drain.

Toss the greens with the vinaigrette in a large bowl. To serve, evenly divide the greens on small plates, and top each serving with the cherries, apples, blue cheese, and pecans.

*As the days grow short, some faces grow long. But not mine. Every autumn, when the wind turns cold and darkness comes early, I am suddenly happy. It's time to start making soup again.*
—Leslie Newman

### Tips for Making an
# Autumn Party Special

- Print your invitations on beautiful autumn-themed paper. With a hot glue gun, attach the invitation to a tiny baby pumpkin or gourd. Tie the stem with some strips of raffia and hand deliver.

- Use bales of hay as makeshift benches, and cover them with a checkered picnic tablecloth.

- Decorate the table with cutlery and tableware in fall colors. Place gourds, pumpkins, and Indian corn in a centerpiece with festive fall mums and dahlias.

- Let your guests bob for apples like they did when they were kids. Put a sticker on the bottom of one apple. Whichever guest gets that apple takes home a nice bottle of wine as a gift.

- When autumn leaves are abundant, gather up the most colorful ones and place them in the bottom of a glass centerpiece.

- A large hollowed-out jack-o'-lantern pumpkin makes a great soup tureen.

- Make autumn luminarias by hollowing out tiny pumpkins. Scrape out the pulp and place a votive candle inside. Arrange them in groups of three or five for a dramatic effect. Using a white pumpkin or two adds drama.

- Hang autumn leaves with delicate gold thread from a chandelier. The effect is stunning.

- Try this for your place settings: using a gold marker, write the names of each guest on an autumn leaf, and gently place them in each guest's empty water goblet.

# Port-Braised Lamb Shanks

*Braising is our favorite cooking method, especially when we have a group of friends coming over for dinner on a chilly autumn night. Braising has many advantages: it takes a rather inexpensive cut of meat and turns it into something out-of-this world succulent; your house smells amazing while the food is cooking; and you can braise a large amount of food at a time—all perfect for entertaining. This recipe calls for the preparation of a spice rub to coat the lamb shanks. This may sound like a lot of extra work, but don't cut corners by skipping this step—it really makes the dish. The sauce can be served two ways: chunky, with all the delicious braised vegetables, or, if you prefer a more elegant presentation for your guests, go that one extra step and make a silky-smooth sauce. Note: Make sure you have a large enough pot, Dutch oven, or roasting pan for braising all the lamb shanks at once.*

Makes 8 servings

1 tablespoon fennel seeds
½ tablespoon allspice berries
½ tablespoon black peppercorns
1 teaspoon ground cloves
1 teaspoon ground cinnamon
1 teaspoon coarse salt
Eight 1-pound lamb shanks
2 tablespoons extra-virgin olive oil
1 large onion, cut into ½-inch dice (about 2 cups)
2 large carrots, cut into ½-inch dice (about 1 cup)
2 ribs celery, cut into ½-inch dice (about 1 cup)
¾ cup tomato paste
1 tablespoon all-purpose flour
10 cloves garlic, crushed
3 anchovy fillets
6 sprigs fresh thyme
2 bay leaves
Zest from 2 large lemons (about 2 tablespoons)
2 cups ruby port
2 cups chicken broth

Adjust the oven rack to the middle position, and preheat the oven to 300°F.

Mix the fennel, allspice, and peppercorns in small, heavy skillet. Toast on medium-high heat until aromatic, about 2 minutes. Transfer the seeds to a spice grinder and process until finely ground. In small bowl, combine the fennel mixture with the cloves, cinnamon, and salt. Rub each shank with 1 teaspoon of the spice blend and set aside.

Heat the oil in a heavy large, wide pot over medium-high heat. Add the shanks, in batches, until browned on all sides, about 12 minutes per batch. Transfer the shanks to a large platter and set aside.

Reduce the heat to medium and add the onion, carrots, celery, and tomato paste to the pot. Cook, stirring occasionally, until the vegetables begin to soften and brown, about 12 to 15 minutes. Stir in the flour and cook for 1 minute. Stir in the garlic, anchovies, thyme, bay leaves, and lemon zest and cook until fragrant, about 30 seconds. Add the port and broth, scraping the bottom of the pan with a wooden spoon to loosen any browned bits, and bring the mixture to a boil. Return the shanks to the pot, or, if they do not fit, put them with the braising liquid in a large roasting pan, cover tightly with a lid or foil, and braise the lamb until tender, about 2 hours.

If you are making this ahead, you can uncover the pot at this point, let the lamb cool slightly, then put the pot in the refrigerator until cool. Then cover the pot and let it sit in the refrigerator for up to 2 days. Remove any fat from the surface and rewarm the lamb and liquid over low heat for 20 minutes.

If you'd prefer a more elegant, smooth sauce, transfer the shanks to a large dish and tent them with foil to keep warm. Over high heat, whisk the braising mixture until the vegetables break down and the sauce thickens, about 10 minutes. Strain the hot cooking liquid into a saucepan, pressing on the solids to extract as much liquid as possible. Discard the solids and season the sauce with additional salt and pepper if desired.

# Fontina and Thyme Polenta

*Dina did not grow up eating polenta, and the first time she tried it at a restaurant, she wasn't terribly impressed. But when she joined our cooking club, we began to try all different kinds of polenta dishes made with a variety of cheeses, herbs, and liquids. This one is her favorite. It is important to prepare this dish right before serving.*

Makes 8 servings

> 4 cups whole milk
> 4 cups low-sodium chicken broth
> 6 cloves garlic, minced
> 2 teaspoons minced fresh thyme
> 1 teaspoon salt
> 1 teaspoon freshly ground black pepper
> 2 cups polenta
> 2 cups grated fontina cheese (about 8 ounces)
> ½ cup freshly grated Parmigiano-Reggiano cheese (about 2 ounces)

Combine the milk, broth, garlic, thyme, salt, and pepper in a large, heavy saucepan and bring to a boil over medium-high heat. Lower the heat to medium and slowly whisk in the polenta. Whisking constantly, cook until the polenta is thick and creamy, about 15 minutes. Remove the saucepan from the heat, add the fontina and Parmigiano-Reggiano, and stir until the cheeses are melted. Season with additional salt and pepper, if desired, and serve immediately.

# Roasted Brussels Sprouts with Pancetta and Shallots

*When hosting a cooking club dinner, we give some thought to how the house will smell as people walk in the door. Whether it is the tantalizing aroma of a dish braising in the oven, a freshly baked dessert, or candles burning around the house, we want the house to smell cozy and warm and delicious. Brussels sprouts are the perfect autumn vegetable, but when steamed or boiled, they often smell sort of, well, stinky. But when you roast them, Brussels sprouts become golden and caramelized, and they smell just heavenly. They taste even better, too.*

2 tablespoons extra-virgin olive oil

6 ounces sliced pancetta or bacon, cut into ¼-inch dice

8 shallots, thinly sliced

2 pounds Brussels sprouts, trimmed and cut in half

1 teaspoon coarse salt

½ teaspoon freshly ground black pepper

2½ tablespoons balsamic vinegar

2½ tablespoons freshly squeezed lemon juice (about 1 lemon)

Preheat the oven to 425°F.

Heat the oil over medium-high heat in a large skillet, add the pancetta, and cook until browned and crisp. Remove the pancetta and allow it to drain on a paper towel. Reduce the heat to medium and add the sliced shallots to the pan. Cook until softened and slightly golden brown, about 8 to 10 minutes. Add the Brussels sprouts, salt, and pepper to the shallots and toss to combine. Spread the mixture on a large baking sheet.

Roast the Brussels sprouts in the hot oven for 10 minutes, then sprinkle with the balsamic vinegar. Shake the pan a little bit to brown the sprouts evenly, and return them to the oven for 10 or 15 minutes more until the vegetables are cooked through and golden brown.

Remove the pan from the oven, sprinkle the sprouts with lemon juice, and transfer them to a serving bowl. Top with the pancetta. Serve warm or at room temperature.

# Gingerbread Cupcakes with Lemon Cream and Candied Pistachio Sprinkles

*Gingerbread and fall are synonymous for us. When we bake for our families, we like to keep it pure and simple: just a piece of warm gingerbread with some powdered sugar sprinkled on top. But when we entertain, we like to do something a bit more fun and special. Cupcakes bring out the child in all of us, and the pistachio sprinkles add a nice crunch to the luscious, creamy topping. For cooking club, these cupcakes can be frosted and transported in a cupcake holder, or baked ahead and frosted at the host's home.*

Makes 22 small cupcakes

¼ pound (1 stick) unsalted butter at room temperature
1 cup packed light brown sugar
3 eggs
2 cups all-purpose flour
1 tablespoon ground ginger
1½ teaspoons baking soda
1 teaspoon ground cinnamon
½ teaspoon ground cloves
¼ teaspoon grated nutmeg
¼ teaspoon salt
1 cup molasses
1 cup dark beer, such as Guinness stout
2 teaspoons lemon zest
Lemon Cream (recipe follows)
Candied Pistachios (recipe follows)

Preheat the oven to 350°F. Line a 12-cup muffin pan with 12 paper liners, and place 10 paper liners inside another muffin pan.

Using an electric mixer, cream together the butter and sugar in a large bowl until fluffy, about 2 minutes. Beat in the eggs 1 at a time.

In a medium-size bowl, sift together the flour, ginger, baking soda, cinnamon, cloves, nutmeg, and salt.

In a small bowl, combine the molasses, beer, and lemon zest.

Slowly add ⅓ of the flour mixture to the butter and egg mixture and mix. Add ⅓ of the beer and molasses mixture and mix. Continue adding the ingredients alternately, mixing just until they are incorporated. Be careful not to overmix the batter.

Fill the prepared pans halfway with the batter and bake for 20 minutes or until a toothpick inserted in the center of the cupcakes comes out clean. Transfer pans to a rack and cool for 15 minutes.

Frost the cupcakes with the Lemon Cream and sprinkle them with the Candied Pistachios. Refrigerate until ready to serve.

## Lemon Cream

Makes 3 cups

> 1 cup heavy cream, well chilled
> One 10-ounce jar (1¼ cups) lemon curd

Beat the cream with the electric mixer until soft peaks form. Gently fold in the lemon curd until thoroughly combined. Cover and refrigerate, up to a day in advance, until ready to use.

## Candied Pistachios

Makes ½ cup

> ¼ cup sugar
> ½ cup chopped toasted pistachios

Line a baking sheet with a silicone baking mat or a piece of parchment paper, and set aside. Cook the sugar in a small, heavy skillet over medium-high heat until the sugar melts and turns a deep golden-brown color, about 2 or 3 minutes. Remove from the heat and add the pistachios, stirring to coat. Pour the nuts out onto the prepared baking sheet. With 2 forks, quickly separate the pistachios pieces, creating small clumps of pistachio sprinkles. Cool completely. The nuts can be prepared in advance and stored at room temperature in an airtight container for up to 1 week.

# The Stone Soup Cooking Club

*Recipes You Will Try Only Once* is the name of the cookbook the Stone Soup Cooking Club founder, Millie Schwartz, would write if she had the opportunity, says Joyce Grover, a member of the cooking club for more than fifteen years.

"Our club has been cooking together for over twenty-five years. We all have vast collections of cookbooks and recipes, and we've tried hundreds of them. Many recipes have turned out so well that they go straight into our repertoire of recipes; and others, well, they are recipes you will try only once—and we have enough of those to fill a book," says Grover.

The Stone Soup Cooking Club of Plattsburgh, New York, consists of twenty-four members, all between the ages of 50 and 90. Grover, who is 86, says, "We have made a conscious effort to keep it just ladies. But once a year, we have a summer picnic where husbands are invited."

The group meets the second Tuesday of every month, from September through May, and it is always a luncheon meeting. At the May meetings, all twenty-four members sign up for committees of four members each and decide which committee will host which month's luncheon. One person on the committee hosts the luncheon, and the other three members cook, prepare the menus and invitations, and help clean up.

"I think one of my favorite parts of being in a cooking club like ours is that we can see how other people set up their kitchens, how they store things, how they circulate—it is very enlightening," says Grover. "And being on a committee is wonderful, because we are working as a team while getting ready to entertain a large group."

All the luncheons are sit-down, not buffet style, according to Grover, and the committee serves the food. Once the luncheon is over, the group gathers for about an hour afterward to discuss the recipes, go over the menu, and pass on information for locating hard-to-find ingredients. Then they open up the discussion to anything related to food. "I have learned the most during these discussions, and it's where I get the best cooking tips, and great restaurant tips, too," says Grover. "At one of our meetings, someone said that she had just heard about a woman who was starting to teach Italian cooking classes. A group of us decided to go, and we had the best time."

The Stone Soup Cooking Club has written guidelines that are distributed to members when they join. The names of people wishing to become members are added to a list, and new members are accepted according to the order in which they were added. There is a fifty dollar annual membership fee that goes toward the food for the year's luncheons and also pays for the meat served at the summer picnic. If the cost for the luncheons goes over the allocated amount, the committee absorbs the cost.

The group's playful and creative side becomes evident as Grover talks about all the different themes throughout the years. There was an April Fool's luncheon, where everything was backwards—the meal began with dessert. Then there was the potato-themed luncheon, where everyone was given a Mr. Potato Head toy as a party favor. There was the "cooking with herbs" theme, for which the committee prepared little jars of herbal jelly for everyone to take home to enjoy. And then there was the Mardi Gras theme, where the person who won the ring from the kings' cake had to host the summer picnic.

Here's one of their sample menus, from a Halloween-themed "Bone Appetit" luncheon. For that event, the Butternut Squash and Apple Soup became the Smoking Cauldron Squash Soup; Roasted Red Pepper Tomato Sauce was Devils and Demons Sauce; Three-Beet Caviar Salad with Endive and Goat Cheese became Vampire Beet Salad; and everything was served with Sinister Cider. The committee members dressed as witches, with wigs and pointy black hats.

"We tend to go all out with our themes—it's one of the best parts of being in a cooking club," says Grover. The international themes are some of the most difficult, because all the members of the Stone Soup Cooking Club live in a small town without much access to international restaurants and markets.

"That doesn't stop us, though," says Grover, as she talks about the time she and her committee drove to Montreal to research a Portuguese-themed club luncheon. They ate at a Portuguese restaurant and then shopped at a Portuguese market for ingredients. "That was a really great learning experience," says Grover. "The only thing that didn't seem to go over very well was an appetizer made with salted cod. Otherwise, we did a tremendous job."

Then there was the time they drove to a Thai restaurant in Burlington, Vermont. "We must have asked the waitress a hundred questions, and as we were leaving, she looked at us and said, 'You're very brave.'"

*Holy Mole!*
*Latin American Cuisine*

*Hear the Music and Feel the Beat*

*You're Invited to Sample Some Great Latin Eats*

*Join Me As We Celebrate the Foods of Latin America*

*Menu*

Watermelon Mojitos

Swiss Chard and Chorizo Empanadas

Salvadoran Pupusas with Shrimp Ceviche Slaw

Yucatan Lime Soup

Orange and Jicama Salad with Baby Spinach

Poblano Pepper and Cilantro Quinoa

Kickin' Chicken Mole

Mexican Chocolate Sorbet

# Watermelon Mojitos

*Before Hurricane Katrina hit, we used to go to New Orleans every year for the French Quarter Festival with our husbands. During one of our visits, we had a wonderful meal at a restaurant called Jacquimo's, which was recommended to us by Anthony Bourdain (sigh) via his television show. When Bourdain tells you to go somewhere to eat, neither of us questions it—we just go. Our husbands patiently put up with this Bourdain obsession of ours, and this time they were incredibly grateful. While waiting for our table, we sat at the bar and ordered watermelon mojitos. They were so good that we ordered another round, and this time we watched the bartender intently as she prepared them. We don't know what the bartender thought of us staring at her, but our cooking club members are very grateful for our version of this amazing cocktail.*

Makes 8 mojitos

2 cups sugar
1 cup water

One 5-pound seedless watermelon, peeled and cut into forty-eight 1-inch cubes
1 large bunch mint, leaves removed, plus 8 sprigs of mint
8 tablespoons simple syrup (recipe follows)
1 cup freshly squeezed lime juice (about 8 limes)
2 cups light rum
Ice cubes
2 cups seltzer or sparkling water

A few hours ahead, make a simple syrup by putting the sugar and water in a small saucepan. Stirring occasionally, bring the syrup to a boil over medium-high heat. As soon as the sugar dissolves completely, remove the syrup from the heat and chill thoroughly. The syrup can be stored in the refrigerator for up to 1 week.

When you are ready to serve the mojitos, place 6 watermelon cubes in each of eight 12-ounce glasses. Top each glass with 6 mint leaves that have been roughly torn by hand. Using a muddler or the end of a wooden spoon, crush the watermelon and bruise the mint leaves for about 20 seconds (don't crush them any longer or the mint will become bitter).

For each mojito, add 1 tablespoon simple syrup, 2 tablespoons lime juice, and ¼ cup rum to the glass. Fill the glass to just below the rim with ice, pour into a shaker, and shake vigorously for 30 seconds. Pour the mojito mixture back into the glass, top off with ¼ cup seltzer or sparkling water, and garnish with a sprig of mint. Repeat for each cocktail and serve immediately.

# Swiss Chard and Chorizo Empanadas

*Dina hosted a Latin American–themed cooking club dinner one year, which ended up being one of her favorites in part because of the empanadas. We made Swiss Chard Empanadas from Susan Feniger and Mary Sue Milliken's* Cantina *cookbook. Their recipe calls for a pastry dough, which is very common for empanadas, and if you're a purist, is the way to go. Our version uses puff pastry, and we added some Spanish chorizo to the filling, which adds a salty flavor and crispy texture to the sweet and buttery Swiss chard.*

Makes 12 servings

1 pound Swiss chard
2 tablespoons extra-virgin olive oil
3 ounces Spanish chorizo (cured spiced pork sausage), finely chopped (about ¾ cup)
1 large onion, finely chopped
3 cloves garlic, minced
1 teaspoon dried oregano
½ teaspoon ground cumin
½ teaspoon salt
½ teaspoon freshly ground black pepper
1 cup grated Monterey Jack cheese

2 sheets (one 17.3-ounce package) frozen puff pastry, thawed according to package directions
1 large egg beaten with 1 teaspoon water for egg wash

To make the filling, cut the chard leaves into small pieces and put them in a large bowl. Cut the stems into ½-inch dice and put them in separate bowl.

Heat the oil in a large skillet over medium-high heat. Add the chorizo and cook for 5 minutes, stirring frequently, until the chorizo is crispy. Transfer the chorizo to a small bowl with a slotted spoon.

Add the onion to the skillet and sauté until soft, about 5 minutes. Add the garlic, oregano, and cumin and cook for 30 seconds. Add the chard stems and cook for 6 minutes, until they begin to soften. Add a portion of the chard leaves, adding the rest in batches as they wilt down and space becomes available in the skillet. Add the salt and pepper and cook, stirring, until the chard is tender and the liquid has evaporated, about 4 to 5 minutes. Return the chorizo to the skillet and remove it from the heat. Let the filling cool to room temperature, then stir in the Monterey Jack.

Roll out 1 puff pastry sheet on a lightly floured work surface. Cut the pastry with a biscuit or cookie cutter to make six 3½-inch rounds. Brush the borders of the rounds with the egg wash and place 1½ tablespoons of filling in the center of each round. Fold the dough over and crimp the edges with a fork to seal. Repeat the process with the second sheet of puff pastry.

Arrange the 12 empanadas on a greased baking sheet, placing each empanada about 1 inch apart, and chill for 30 minutes, or up to 1 day ahead. At this point, you can freeze the empanadas in a single layer. Once they are completely frozen, put them in freezer bags. They can be kept in the freezer up to 1 month.

Preheat the oven to 350°F.

Just before baking, brush the empanadas with the egg wash, and using a small sharp knife, cut 2 or 3 small slits in the top of each one to allow steam to escape. Bake them until golden and crispy, about 20 minutes, or for 25 minutes if frozen. The empanadas can be served warm or at room temperature.

*The only real stumbling block is fear of failure. In cooking you've got to have a what-the-hell attitude.*

—Julia Child

## Tips for a Successful
# Latin American–Inspired Dinner

- String paper placemats in rows from the ceiling, to imitate the traditional paper-cuts you see in Mexican restaurants. Placemats can be purchased very inexpensively at party stores.

- Hang a sombrero over the back of each guest's chair.

- For place settings, write each guest's name with a gold or silver marker on a terra cotta pot that contains a small cactus plant.

- Use a Mexican blanket or other textiles for a table runner or as part of your centerpiece.

- Hire a local mariachi band to play while your guests are enjoying their appetizers.

- Piñatas aren't just for kids. Fill a piñata with items an adult would enjoy, like good-quality chocolates and other Latin American candies, or mini bottles of alcohol, and let the adults get their aggressions out while acting like kids.

- As a party favor, fill decorative margarita glasses with Mexican chocolates, chili peppers, or pepitas.

- Arrange "Day of the Dead" figurines throughout your table setting.

- Play music by your favorite Latin American singer or group as your guests arrive.

- Set a variety of miniature bottles of hot sauce at each place setting for guests to take home with them.

- Paper flowers hung decoratively from the ceiling add huge bursts of color and are easy and inexpensive to make, or you can purchase them from a craft store.

# Salvadoran Pupusas with Shrimp Ceviche Slaw

*Berkeley, California, has an annual food festival called* Spice of Life, *with cooking demonstrations by local restaurant chefs and vendors offering all kinds of delicious international foods. One year our friend and fellow cooking club member Cindy LaCasse went with Dina to the festival together with their families, and Cindy insisted on standing in a very long line at a Salvadoran food vendor's stall. They were running late, but Cindy just gave Dina that "trust me" look and waited patiently for what turned out to be a very special dish:* pupusas, *lightly griddled masa corn pancakes stuffed with oozing cheese. Pupusas are traditionally served with a spicy cabbage slaw called* curtido, *but for a special cooking club gathering, try them with this shrimp ceviche slaw.*

Makes 16 appetizer servings

> 2 cups instant masa harina (corn tortilla flour), such as Maseca
> 1 teaspoon baking powder
> ½ teaspoon salt
> 1½ cups warm water
> 1 cup freshly grated *queso fresco* or mozzarella cheese
> Vegetable oil for oiling the skillet
> Shrimp Ceviche Slaw (recipe follows)
> Fresh cilantro sprigs for garnish

Combine the masa harina, baking powder, and salt in a large mixing bowl or the bowl of an electric stand mixer fitted with a dough hook. Add the water and mix until a dough forms, about 1 minute. Knead the dough by hand for 2 minutes, or with the dough hook for 1 minute. The dough should be moist but not sticky, and it should not crack at the edges when you press on it. If necessary, stir a little more masa harina  or water into the dough, 1 tablespoon at a time. Cover with a kitchen towel and set the dough aside to rest for 10 minutes.

Divide the dough into 16 golf ball–size balls. Place them on a tray and cover with a clean damp kitchen towel to prevent them from drying out. Take a ball of dough in the palm of your hand (it is easier to work the dough if you lightly oil your palms with a little vegetable oil first). Press your thumb in the center of the dough ball to make an indentation and work it with your fingers until you form a concave disk with walls that are about ¼ inch thick. When it is formed, it should look like an artichoke bottom.

Place about 1 tablespoon of queso fresco on each disk, then pinch the dough together to enclose and form a ball. Press out the ball with your palms to form a 2¼-inch disk. Be careful that the cheese doesn't spill out. Place the ball on the tray and cover it with the damp towel. Repeat for all 16 of the dough balls. At this point, the pupusas can be stored in an airtight container and chilled for up to 2 hours before cooking.

Heat a large cast-iron or nonstick skillet over medium-high heat. Brush the skillet lightly with oil and cook each pupusa for 1 or 2 minutes on each side until golden brown. Remove the cooked pupusas to a plate, cover, and keep warm in a warm oven until all the pupusas are done.

To serve, spoon a heaping teaspoon of the Shrimp Ceviche Slaw onto each hot pupusa and garnish with sprigs of cilantro.

## Shrimp Ceviche Slaw
Makes 2 cups or enough for 16 appetizer servings

½ pound medium-size shrimp (15 to 25 shrimp), peeled and deveined
½ cup finely shredded cabbage
¼ cup diced red onion
¼ seedless English cucumber (usually sold wrapped in plastic), cut in half lengthwise, cored, and diced (about ½ cup)
¼ cup diced peeled jicama
½ jalapeño pepper, seeded and chopped
¼ cup freshly squeezed lime juice (about 2 limes)
1 tablespoon vinegary Mexican bottled hot sauce such as Cholula
1 tablespoon extra-virgin olive oil
½ teaspoon salt
⅛ teaspoon ground cumin
¼ cup chopped fresh cilantro
1 large ripe avocado, peeled, pitted, and cut into ¼-inch cubes

Bring 1 quart salted water to a boil in a large pot. Add the shrimp to the water and poach them uncovered for just 30 seconds and drain. Coarsely chop the shrimp and set aside.

In a large bowl, add the cabbage, red onion, cucumber, jicama, jalapeño, lime juice, Mexican hot sauce, olive oil, salt, and cumin and toss gently until well mixed. Mix in the shrimp and let marinate in the refrigerator, covered, for at least 3 hours or up to 8 hours to allow the flavors to develop.

Just before serving, gently stir the cilantro and avocado into the shrimp mixture.

# Yucatan Lime Soup

*This warming soup, which Dina learned from her good friend Heather Bondy, is wonderful on a cold, rainy day. Full of tender, shredded chicken in a flavorful lime-accented broth, this will be one of those dishes you make time and time again. We like to serve this soup with brown rice, but feel free to use white rice or even orzo.*

Makes 8 servings

Eight 4-inch corn tortillas
½ cup vegetable oil
Salt
1 large onion, chopped
1 jalapeño pepper with the seeds, thinly sliced
6 cloves garlic, minced
2 large tomatoes, cut in half crosswise, seeded
Two 6- to 8-ounce skinless, boneless chicken breasts
2½ quarts chicken stock, preferably homemade
1½ teaspoons dried oregano
1 teaspoon freshly cracked black pepper
Juice of 6 fresh limes (about ⅔ cup)
2 cups cooked brown rice
1 large avocado, diced
¼ cup chopped fresh cilantro

Cut the tortillas into ¼-inch strips. Heat the oil in a large skillet over high heat. Fry the tortilla strips in batches until golden brown on both sides, 3 to 5 minutes, adding more oil if needed. Drain the strips on paper towels. Season while still warm with salt to taste.

Remove all but 2 tablespoons of the oil from the skillet. Add the onion and jalapeño. Sauté until the onions begin to soften and turn slightly golden, about 4 minutes. Add the garlic and sauté for 30 seconds. Remove the pan from the heat and set aside.

Working over a small bowl, grate each tomato half on the coarse side of a box grater. Discard the tomato skin, and set the grated tomatoes aside.

Put the chicken breasts and stock in large saucepan. Bring the stock nearly to a boil—do not allow the stock to boil. Reduce the heat to medium-low, and skim off and discard any foam. Add the oregano and pepper and cook for 15 minutes, or until the meat is tender.

Remove the chicken from the soup and set aside until it is cool enough to handle. When the chicken has cooled a bit, shred it into bite-size pieces. Set the chicken aside.

Add the onion mixture, tomatoes, and lime juice to the stock, and let it simmer over medium heat for 10 minutes. Add the shredded chicken and cook for another 5 minutes, or until the chicken is heated through. Season the soup to taste with salt.

To serve, spoon ¼ cup of rice into each soup bowl. Ladle the soup over the rice and garnish with a handful of the tortilla strips, diced avocado, and a sprinkling of cilantro. Serve immediately.

# Orange and Jicama Salad with Baby Spinach

*Dina's mom always used to say, "The eyes eat before the mouth," and this salad makes her case. The colors are bright and vibrant and fresh in presentation when combined. This is one of our favorite salads to prepare and serve because it combines sweet, sour, and spicy flavors with soft and crunchy textures, and it all works wonderfully together.*

Makes 8 servings

> 6 small navel oranges
> 1 jalapeño pepper, seeded and minced
> ¼ cup chopped fresh cilantro
> 3 tablespoons freshly squeezed lime juice (about 1½ limes)
> ¼ cup extra-virgin olive oil
> ¼ teaspoon salt plus additional as needed
> ¼ teaspoon freshly ground black pepper plus additional as needed
> 1 large jicama (about 1 pound), peeled and cut into matchsticks
> 1 small red onion, thinly sliced
> 10 ounces fresh baby spinach
> 2 large California avocadoes, cut in half and thinly sliced

Peel the oranges. Working over a large bowl to catch the juice, cut sections free from the membranes. Reserve 3 tablespoons of orange juice for the vinaigrette.

In a small bowl, whisk together the jalapeño, cilantro, lime juice, oil, salt, pepper, and orange juice.

Toss the jicama, orange segments, red onion, and spinach with the vinaigrette in a large bowl.

Arrange the orange and jicama mixture on salad plates. Top with the avocado slices. Drizzle any remaining vinaigrette over the salads, season with salt and pepper to taste, and serve.

# Poblano Pepper and Cilantro Quinoa

*Quinoa is an ancient plant that originated in the Andean region of South America. Although it cooks up like a grain, it is the seeds of the plant that are used. Until recently you could find quinoa only in health food stores, but now it's widely available. Not only is quinoa delicious, it is also high in protein and fiber, gluten-free, fast-cooking, and very nutritious. If you haven't yet tried it, this recipe is a great way to start your own love affair with quinoa. Note: Rinse quinoa thoroughly in a fine-mesh sieve with cold water before cooking, otherwise it will have an unpleasant bitter flavor.*

Makes 8 servings

  1 tablespoon vegetable oil
  ½ cup chopped shallots
  2 fresh poblano chili peppers, stemmed, seeded, and chopped
  3 cloves garlic, minced
  1 teaspoon ground cumin
  1½ teaspoons salt
  ½ teaspoon freshly ground black pepper
  2 cups quinoa, rinsed thoroughly and drained
  4 cups chicken stock
  ¼ cup chopped fresh cilantro leaves

Heat the oil in a large saucepan over medium-high heat until hot. Add the shallots and poblanos and cook, stirring, for 3 minutes, until the vegetables have softened. Add the garlic, cumin, salt, and pepper and cook, stirring, for 30 seconds. Add the quinoa and stock and bring to a boil. Cover, reduce the heat, and simmer for about 15 to 20 minutes or until the quinoa opens up into little spirals and you can see the little white ring around each flake. The quinoa should not be mushy. Remove the pan from the heat and let it sit, covered, for 10 minutes. Fold in the cilantro and fluff gently with a fork. Serve immediately.

# Kickin' Chicken Mole

*Our families went on vacation one year to Mexico's Yucatan Peninsula, and we came back completely inspired by the food. Michelle immediately wanted to host a Mexican-themed cooking club dinner, and she assigned Dina the chicken mole. Dina found out the hard way that making mole can be a very long process: Her recipe took three days to prepare! But it is one of those unforgettable dishes, and she began a mission to find a way to make a quicker mole that would still keep the rich flavors intact. The spiciness of the chili peppers mixed with the sweetness of the chocolate, fruit, and nuts make for an intensely flavorful sauce. If your grocery store does not carry the chiles, you should be able to find them at a Mexican market. The mole can be prepared up to two days in advance and refrigerated, which is great for entertaining.*

Makes 8 servings

8 pounds skinless bone-in chicken thighs
2½ quarts water
1 large onion, peeled and quartered
1 whole head garlic, outer skin removed, cut in half crosswise
1½ teaspoons salt

---

½ cup prunes
½ cup raisins
8 dried *mulato* chili peppers, stemmed, seeds and membranes removed
6 dried pasilla chili peppers, stemmed, seeds and membranes removed
5 dried ancho chili peppers, stemmed, seeds and membranes removed
½ cup sliced toasted almonds
¼ cup dry-roasted unsalted peanuts
¼ cup plus 1 tablespoon sesame seeds, toasted
1 small ripe banana
One 14.5-ounce can diced tomatoes, drained
6 whole cloves garlic, peeled
2 teaspoons ground cinnamon
1 teaspoon ground cloves
1 teaspoon ground allspice
1 teaspoon dried Mexican oregano

1 teaspoon dried thyme

1 teaspoon ground cumin

1½ teaspoons salt

6 ounces Mexican chocolate such as Ibarra

½ cup dark brown sugar

To cook the chicken, put the chicken thighs, water, onion, garlic, and salt in a large pot and bring it nearly to a boil. Reduce the heat to medium-low, and skim and discard any foam. Cover and simmer until the chicken is tender, about 35 minutes. Transfer the chicken to platter. Strain the broth into a large bowl and set aside. There should be about 10 cups of broth. Discard the solids.

To prepare the mole sauce, put the prunes and raisins in a small bowl. Add 1 cup of the reserved hot chicken broth and cover. Set the dried fruit aside to let it soften and plump in the broth.

Place the mulato, pasilla, and ancho chili peppers in a saucepan, cover with 5 cups of reserved broth, and bring to a boil. Lower the heat to a simmer and cook until tender, about 35 minutes.

While the chiles are cooking, put the almonds, peanuts, and the ¼ cup of sesame seeds into a blender jar with 1 cup of reserved chicken broth and blend until smooth. Strain the nut and seed mixture through a fine-mesh sieve into a heavy pot. Set over low heat and simmer.

Put the prune and raisin mixture, banana, tomatoes, garlic, cinnamon, cloves, allspice, oregano, thyme, cumin, and salt in the blender with 1 cup of broth. Blend until smooth. Strain through the fine-mesh sieve into the pot with the nut mixture. Continue to simmer the mixture.

Put the chili pepper mixture with the cooking liquid in the blender, add an additional cup of broth, and blend until smooth. Strain the puréed chiles through a fine-mesh sieve into the pot with the fruit and nut mixture. Add the last remaining cup of chicken broth. Cook, uncovered, over low heat for 40 minutes, stirring often.

Add the chocolate and brown sugar to the mole; simmer over low heat for 10 minutes, stirring often. At this point, the mole and the chicken can be brought to room temperature and chilled in the refrigerator for up to 2 days. Just before serving, bring mole to a gentle simmer over medium heat, add the chicken thighs, and cook until the chicken is heated through, about 10 to 15 minutes.

To serve, arrange the chicken pieces on a platter. Spoon the mole sauce over the chicken and sprinkle with the remaining tablespoon of sesame seeds. Serve immediately.

# Mexican Chocolate Sorbet

*Technically this isn't really a sorbet, since the recipe has egg yolks in it. But the eggs give this dessert a smooth, velvety texture that is simply sublime. If you are bringing this dessert to a cooking club gathering, we recommend that you make the custard at home, giving it a chance to chill for at least four hours and preferably even overnight. Then take the custard and your ice cream maker with you and finish it at the host's house. Make sure the ice cream canister goes immediately into the host's freezer when you arrive. The sorbet is at its best when served immediately, right out of the ice cream machine, but if you freeze it at home, allow it to temper for awhile at your host's home before serving, either in the refrigerator or on the counter.*

Makes 1 quart or enough for 8 servings

> 3½ disks (11 ounces) Mexican chocolate such as Ibarra
> 3 cups water
> 1 cup sugar
> ⅛ teaspoon cayenne pepper
> ⅛ teaspoon salt
> 4 egg yolks
> 1 teaspoon pure vanilla extract

Put the chocolate, water, sugar, cayenne, and salt in a heavy medium-size saucepan. Whisk together over medium heat until the chocolate has completely melted and the mixture is smooth, about 10 to 12 minutes.

Whisk the egg yolks in a large bowl until well blended. Very slowly, add half the chocolate mixture to the yolks while whisking quickly to temper the yolks. Whisk the yolk mixture back into the saucepan with the remaining chocolate mixture, and stir them together over medium heat until the custard thickens slightly, about

5 minutes. Do not boil the custard. Remove the custard from the heat and stir in the vanilla.

Pour the custard through a fine-mesh sieve into a plastic container and cover tightly. Refrigerate until the mixture is completely chilled, at least 4 and preferably 8 to 12 hours. Freeze the sorbet in an ice cream maker according to the manufacturer's instructions. If you are not serving it immediately, transfer the sorbet to a plastic container and keep in the freezer until nearly ready to serve.

# The S & M Club

Marlies Roberts and her friend were discussing their obsession with food and Netflix one afternoon and decided to do something constructive about it. So they started The S&M Club. No, Roberts tells us, not *that* kind of S&M. In this case, S&M stands for "supper and movie."

Roberts' friend has since moved, but the cooking and movie club has grown to twelve members, all of whom live within a few miles of downtown Boston. They are all between twenty-three and twenty-eight years old, and they joined the group because they were young and didn't belong to a social circle that regularly gave dinner parties.

"When we first began the club, we invited only some of our close friends who we knew enjoyed cooking. But as time went on, we began to invite other people we have met who share the same love for food, cooking, and movies," says Roberts. "I have a connection to everyone in the group. Some are co-workers, some ex-co-workers, some friends from home, some friends from college, and several friends of friends."

The club formed in September 2006, and they have been meeting monthly since then. All themes are based on a movie. Past themes have included Italian (*The Godfather*), Fall Harvest (*Halloween*), Greek (*My Big Fat Greek Wedding*), Christmas Holiday (*Christmas Vacation*), Southern (*Steel Magnolias*), French (*Amélie*), Irish (*In America*), Indian (*Kal Ho Naa Ho*), Mexican-American (*Real Women Have Curves*), Spanish Tapas (*Pan's Labyrinth*), Hawaiian (*From Here to Eternity*), and Thai (*The Beach*).

The S&M Club always meets on Sundays. Members decide the theme for the following month, as well as the host, during the gathering. "All the host has to do is choose the movie, e-mail the invitation, provide the kitchen, and provide the wine if no one is making a cocktail," says Roberts.

Invitations are handled through Evite.com, an online invitation service. The host sends out the Evite invitation with the theme information, as well as the time and place. The host usually decides on the movie but sometimes will have a poll so members can vote. The menu is not part of the invitation. Once members receive their invitation, they respond with which course they will be preparing—an appetizer, entrée, side dish, salad, or dessert. Each member then researches recipes to go with the theme. Recipes typically are chosen from online recipe sites, although Roberts says one member swears by Rachel Ray.

"Since we do a lot of ethnic dishes to go with the movie, we have had a couple of debacles. Like the time someone was preparing cannoli for dessert for our Italian-themed night but forgot the pastry. We just served the pastry cream in martini glasses, and it was delicious," says Roberts.

"The important thing is to have fun, not be afraid to try new recipes and new foods, and look at this as an opportunity to learn. We are all big movie fans, but we find ourselves trying new and unique recipes and cooking techniques the more we get together. In fact, I think it is what I enjoy most about the club," says Roberts.

For the Indian-themed dinner, the group chose a Bollywood movie, and many members went to the Indian markets around Boston to research ingredients. "That was a lot of fun. I, along with most of the members, really get into the themes. In preparation for the Indian night, I did a lot of Web research on how to prepare traditional Indian dishes, went to an Indian market to purchase all the authentic ingredients, and then spent all day Sunday before the meeting preparing the dish. After all of the effort, it is really rewarding to make something that everyone enjoys. I now know how to prepare several delicious Indian meals. I also enjoy watching my friends, some of whom were previously not adventurous eaters, try out new things," says Roberts.

In order to fit the dinner and movie into one evening, the group typically meets by 6:30 p.m. The members try to bring their dishes as close to ready-to-serve as possible, and do only last-minute finishing touches, if needed, in the host's kitchen. Over drinks and appetizers, the group discusses the food and recipes they used. Following their discussion, everyone digs into the rest of the meal and moves into the living room to watch the movie. "We are usually done by 10 p.m., which is perfect, since we all have to be at work the next day," says Roberts.

Roberts is the coordinator of the group, and she keeps a spreadsheet of all of the past themes, as well as ideas for future themes. "I think if I were going to give advice to anyone who wanted to start a cooking club, it would be keep it organized, make sure there is a lot of communication, and most important, keep it fun."

# Fuzzy Slippers, Chocolate Pudding, and a Warm Fire:
## Comfort Food at its Most Comforting

*You Are Cozily Invited to Enjoy an*
*Evening of Comfort Food*
*Don Your Favorite Pajamas or Sweats and Slippers*
*For a Relaxing Evening by the Fire*

### Menu

Mulled Wine

Marinated Olives with Citrus and Garlic

Spiced Pecans

Iceberg Salad Wedges with Crispy Bacon and Tangy Blue-Cheese Dressing

Gruyère and Rosemary Popovers

Slow-Braised Beef Short Ribs with Red Wine

Buttered Egg Noodles

Creamy Chocolate-Kahlúa Pudding

# Mulled Wine

*This is the perfect drink to sip on a cozy evening in front of a roaring fire. Have the mulled wine ready to serve before the first members arrive so that your house will smell wonderful when they get there. Set out a ladle and some pretty serving cups next to your slow cooker, and allow everyone to help themselves. Make sure you don't boil the wine, as the alcohol will burn off and dilute the flavor, making it taste bitter. This recipe can easily be doubled if you would like to serve more than one glass per guest. Be sure to use a good-quality red wine. Any off flavors from a bad wine will only intensify when heated, so serve up the good stuff.*

Makes 8 servings

> 2 bottles red wine, such as Cotes du Rhône or Cabernet Sauvignon
> 12 whole cloves
> 4 allspice berries
> 4 cinnamon sticks
> ½ cup granulated sugar
> Peel of 1 large orange, white pith removed
> ½ cup dark rum

Put the wine, cloves, allspice, cinnamon, sugar, and orange peel in a large saucepan over medium-high heat, and allow the mixture to come almost to a boil. Just before it starts to bubble, take the mixture off the heat and let the spice mixture steep in the wine for 10 minutes, then add the rum. Strain the mixture into a slow cooker set to warm, and serve.

# Marinated Olives with Citrus and Garlic

*If you want to impress your fellow club members, marinate some olives. These little nibbles go wonderfully with the Spiced Pecans and Mulled Wine, and they'll make you look like a pro in the kitchen. Homemade marinated olives taste so much fresher than the ones sitting in the grocery-store bins, and they are fun and easy to make. Feel free to play around with the varieties of olives you choose. We like a mixture of black and green ones for a pretty presentation in the bowl. Kalamata and picholine are two of our favorites. Don't forget to put out a little bowl for the pits. Make sure to give the olives enough marinating time in the refrigerator, as they taste better the longer they marinate.*

Makes 2 cups or enough for 8 appetizer servings

2 cups assorted green and black olives in brine (not the canned variety)
½ cup extra-virgin olive oil
Zest of 1 large lemon (about 2 teaspoons)
Zest of 1 small orange (about 1 tablespoon)
5 cloves garlic, thinly sliced
1 tablespoon finely chopped fresh rosemary
1 tablespoon finely chopped fresh thyme
½ teaspoon fennel seeds, lightly crushed
1 teaspoon dried basil, crumbled
¼ teaspoon hot red pepper flakes
¼ teaspoon freshly ground black pepper
2 tablespoons balsamic vinegar

Drain the olives and rinse well in cold water. Put the olives in a large bowl. Add the oil, lemon and orange zest, garlic, rosemary, thyme, fennel, basil, and both kinds of pepper, and mix well to combine. Cover the olives tightly and refrigerate for 7 to 10 days. Stir the olives once a day to allow the flavors to develop. Just before serving, drizzle the balsamic vinegar over the olives.

# Spiced Pecans

*We like to have a tasty snack to munch on when we're catching up with all our friends from our cooking club. Pour these nuts fresh out of the oven into a bowl when guests start to arrive, and watch the gang dig in. There wasn't a stray nut left at cooking club, but you can use any leftovers in a salad. These go great with the Harvest Salad with Apples, Pecans, Dried Cherries, and Blue Cheese on page 152.*

Makes 2 cups or enough for 8 appetizer servings

> 1½ tablespoons vegetable oil
> 1 tablespoon Worcestershire sauce
> 1 tablespoon brown sugar
> 2 cups pecan halves
> 1 teaspoon salt
> 1 teaspoon dried thyme
> ½ teaspoon ground cumin
> ½ teaspoon curry powder
> ¼ teaspoon cayenne pepper

Preheat the oven to 325°F.

Put the vegetable oil, Worcestershire sauce, and brown sugar into a medium-size bowl. Add the nuts, salt, thyme, cumin, curry, and cayenne, and stir until the nuts are completely pecans. Turn the pecans out onto a baking sheet, distributing them in a single layer, and toast them in the oven for 15 to 20 minutes, or until lightly toasted and fragrant. Stir once or twice during toasting to keep the nuts from scorching.

# Iceberg Salad Wedges with Crispy Bacon and Tangy Blue-Cheese Dressing

*Iceberg lettuce is sort of the "polyester" of lettuces, but everyone loves a good old-fashioned iceberg salad once in a while. This is comfort food just like you had as a kid, and it will take you right back to Sunday dinners at Aunt Verna's.*

Makes 8 servings

½ cup sour cream
½ cup mayonnaise
8 ounces crumbled blue cheese
4 tablespoons freshly squeezed lemon juice (about 1 ⅓ lemons)
2 tablespoons Dijon mustard
¼ teaspoon freshly ground black pepper
6 to 8 tablespoons milk

½ pound thick-cut pepper bacon
2 heads iceberg lettuce
1 basket small cherry tomatoes, cut in half

To make the dressing, mix together the sour cream, mayonnaise, blue cheese, lemon juice, mustard, and pepper in a small bowl. Thin the dressing with the milk to the desired consistency. Chill until ready to serve.

Cook the bacon until crisp in a medium-size skillet over medium heat, and let it drain on paper towels. Crumble the bacon and reserve.

Cut each head of lettuce into 4 wedges and place each wedge on a serving plate. Top each wedge with some of the dressing, crumbled bacon, and tomatoes.

*Food, like a loving touch or a glimpse of divine power, has that ability to comfort.*

—Norman Kolpas

## Tips for a Successful
# Dinner of Comfort Food

- Invite guests to wear their favorite pair of pajamas for ultimate coziness. Give a prize for the funniest pair of jammies.

- Place the dining table in front of a roaring fire for instant ambience.

- Greet guests with a pair of slippers or cozy socks to slip on their feet.

- Party favors might include a few personal items (such as hand lotion, lip balm, neck pillow, eye mask, or massage oil), with a note saying "Make yourself comfortable."

- Set out some cards with inspiring messages, poems, or quotes referring to comfort. Have guests read them aloud as they wish.

- For a cozy environment, soft lighting and soothing music work wonders.

# Gruyère and Rosemary Popovers

*These satisfying popovers are true comfort food. They should be served right out of the oven, as they don't keep very well, so be sure to enjoy them the day you bake them. We bake these in a regular muffin pan—there's no need for a special popover pan. If you do happen to have one, by all means use it, but note it will make only 8 or 10 popovers.*

Makes 12 popovers

> 1 cup bread flour
> 1 teaspoon salt
> 1 cup whole milk
> 2 large eggs
> Nonstick cooking spray
> 1 cup grated Gruyère cheese
> 2 teaspoons minced fresh rosemary

Preheat the oven to 450°F.

Sift the flour and salt into a medium-size bowl. Whisk together the milk and eggs and incorporate them into the flour mixture, whisking until smooth. The batter will be thin. Let the mixture rest for 15 minutes before proceeding with the recipe.

Put the muffin pan in the oven for 5 minutes, or until it is very hot. Remove the pan from the oven, spray the cups with nonstick cooking spray, and fill them just over half full with batter. Sprinkle each cup with an equal amount of Gruyère and rosemary, return the pan to the oven, and bake the popovers for 15 minutes on the middle rack. Without opening the door, reduce the heat to 350°F and bake for 10 minutes more, or until the popovers are puffed and golden brown. Serve at once.

# Slow-Braised Beef Short Ribs with Red Wine

*Aside from Cindy, none of us are particularly knowledgeable about wine, so Maria hosted an entire cooking club on wine tasting and wine pairing. What a fun night! We all walked away having learned so much from her, and it inspired us to come up with our own dish incorporating wine. This is one of those dishes best prepared the day before to let the flavors develop, which makes it much easier to skim off the accumulated fat from the top.*

Makes 8 servings

    1 tablespoon extra-virgin olive oil
    2 teaspoons salt, plus more to taste
    ½ teaspoon freshly ground black pepper, plus more to taste
    8 pounds individual beef short ribs, trimmed of extra fat
    2 large onions, finely chopped (about 2 cups)
    4 medium carrots, finely chopped (about 1½ cups)
    4 celery ribs, finely chopped (about 2 cups)
    12 whole cloves garlic, peeled
    Zest of 1 medium orange (about 2 tablespoons)
    2 tablespoons all-purpose flour
    2 tablespoons herbes de Provence
    1 tablespoon ground allspice
    2 bay leaves
    2 cups red wine, such as Zinfandel or Syrah
    2 cups beef stock, preferably homemade, or low-salt chicken broth
    4 cups thickly sliced mushrooms
    2 cups kalamata olives, pitted and rinsed
    ½ cup tomato paste
    3 tablespoons balsamic vinegar
    1 tablespoon chopped fresh parsley

Preheat the oven to 300°F.

In a large, heavy-bottomed pot, heat the oil over medium-high heat, and sprinkle the short ribs with the salt and pepper on both sides. Working in batches, brown the ribs on all sides until golden brown, about 10 minutes per batch. Transfer the ribs to a platter.

Pour off all but 2 tablespoons of fat and add the onions, carrots, celery, garlic, orange zest, and flour. Add the herbes de Provence, allspice, and bay leaves. Reduce heat to medium and cook for 15 minutes to lightly brown the vegetables. Stir in the wine, stock, mushrooms, olives, and tomato paste and bring to a boil over high heat, stirring up any browned bits from the bottom of the pan.

Return the short ribs to the pot along with any accumulated juices from the platter, and add enough water to come just below bottom of the ribs. Bring to a boil over high heat.

Cover the pot tightly and transfer it to the oven. Bake until the meat is fork-tender and falling away from the bone, about 2½ to 3 hours.

Transfer the ribs to a deep serving platter and cover tightly with aluminum foil. Remove the bay leaves from the braising liquid and cover tightly. Place the ribs and the liquid into the refrigerator and let them chill overnight.

When ready to serve, skim the fat from the braising liquid. Bring the liquid to a boil over high heat and cook until it thickens to a sauce-like consistency, about 15 to 20 minutes. Return the short ribs to the sauce and heat through.

Just before serving, adjust the seasoning with extra salt and pepper as needed. Drizzle the balsamic vinegar over the ribs and sprinkle them with the parsley. Spoon the short ribs and sauce over the buttered noodles and serve warm.

# Buttered Egg Noodles

*Fellow cooking club member Nicole is a very minimal type person with a "take me as I am" attitude that we love. She wears very little makeup and still looks beautiful. This recipe is similar in that it reminds us that things don't need to be "fussy" to be good. These noodles are good by themselves, and the clean, simple flavors are a hit with the kids.*

Makes 8 servings

12 ounces egg noodles (or no-yolk noodles, as desired)
¼ cup low-salt chicken broth
3 tablespoons unsalted butter
2 tablespoons minced fresh parsley
1 teaspoon garlic salt
¼ teaspoon freshly ground black pepper
1 tablespoon lemon juice (about ½ small lemon)

Boil the noodles in salted water for 10 to 12 minutes and drain thoroughly.

Put the chicken broth in a small saucepan over medium heat and bring it just to a boil.

Put the broth, noodles, butter, parsley, garlic salt, and pepper in a large bowl and mix until well combined. Let noodles sit for a few minutes to absorb the flavors of the broth. Spoon the short ribs and sauce over the noodles and serve warm.

# Creamy Chocolate-Kahlúa Pudding

*Remember the pudding you used to eat at Grandma's house? It was the real thing, not that stuff out of a box. I think we forget how good homemade pudding can be—but let us tell you, store-bought pudding never tasted like this. Using good-quality chocolate and Kahlúa elevates this "kiddie food" to a sublime dessert made especially for adults. Our cooking club loves this creamy, rich pudding; we have to serve it whenever we indulge in a dinner of comfort foods. Valrhona chocolate is widely available now, but if you can't find it, any good-quality bittersweet dark chocolate will do.*

Makes 8 servings

½ cup granulated sugar
4 tablespoons cornstarch
½ teaspoon salt
4 cups half-and-half
2 tablespoons Kahlúa
8 ounces high-quality bittersweet chocolate, such as Valrhona or
   Scharffen Berger, chopped
2 teaspoons pure vanilla extract
Whipped cream (optional)
Chocolate-covered coffee beans (optional)

In a medium-size saucepan, whisk together the sugar, cornstarch, and salt until well combined.

Whisking constantly over medium heat, gradually add the half-and-half, and heat until the mixture thickens and begins to boil, about 10 minutes. Continue whisking while adding the Kahlúa, and allow the mixture to boil for 1 minute more. Remove the pan from the heat and add the chopped chocolate and the vanilla. Let stand for 5 minutes until the chocolate is melted. Stir gently until smooth.

Divide the pudding between 8 small serving dishes. Cover with plastic wrap, placing it directly onto the surface of each pudding so a skin does not form. Refrigerate for at least 30 minutes before serving.

Garnish with whipped cream and a chocolate-covered coffee bean if desired.

# The Kitchen Table Cooking Club

Throughout this book, we have profiled eleven other cooking clubs from around the country, and we wanted to conclude this tribute to cooking clubs by acquainting you with ours, the Kitchen Table Cooking Club. Being part of a cooking club is a wonderful experience based on rewarding friendships and delicious meals. Since 2001, The Kitchen Table Cooking Club has been bonding over food in a way that has created life-long friendships. A club can only be as good as its members, and our group's strength is visible by the imprints we have all left on each other's hearts.

We have learned a thing or two about each other after cooking together all these years. We know that if Carolyn starts laughing too hard, she will invariably start crying instead. We know that if we are steaming a live crab, someone needs to distract Nicole before the crab hits the water so she won't get upset. We know that Cindy always has some interesting fact about wine that we never knew before, and that Maria's sense of optimism knows no bounds. We know that Lisa will talk about how "she isn't a very good cook," and then proceed to make an absolutely delicious meal every time, and yes, it's almost a given that Dina or Michelle will bring up their love of Anthony Bourdain.

Since you've already read quite a bit about our club throughout this book, in the spirit of Melanie Dunea's *My Last Supper: 50 Great Chefs and Their Final Meals/ Portraits, Interviews, and Recipes*, we asked our cooking club members the following questions pertaining to their experiences being in a cooking club.

## What was your favorite cooking club experience?

Dina, member since 2002: The club night that stands out for me is Maria's Moroccan-themed cooking club. It was a total dining experience, from the elaborate invitations, to the colorful chiffon-draped and decorated dining room, to the belly dancer that entertained us, to the incredible meal that followed.

Michelle, member since 2001: My favorite cooking club experience, hands down, is the one where Dina served the most amazing plank-grilled quail, and then asked us if we wanted to actually write a book on the subject. Me, Dina, Maria, and former cooking club member Gretchen Bernsdorff, actually did write a book on plank grilling that we are all very proud of.

Cindy, member since 2004: Michelle's tribute to New Orleans, in which after Hurricane Katrina we each prepared a dish from a famous New Orleans restaurant. The recipes were challenging and things we hadn't tried or prepared before, like Rabbit Etouffee. I had Antoine's Oyster Rockefeller and that was very fun to try and replicate the legendary recipe.

Maria, founder in 2001: Lisa's sushi adventure. Oh what a night! I also loved Carolyn's tribute to Julia Child where I made my first ever chocolate soufflé, which turned out to be easier than I imagined.

Lisa, member since 2003: Maria's Moroccan-themed cooking club.

Carolyn, member since 2001: I've had so many great times. It's difficult to pull one from the last seven years. I always seem to think of Michelle's house and the New Orleans dinner. This was the first dinner we had to be prepared to discuss our chefs. I learned so much that night. The food was out of this world. I tried many things I hadn't in the past. That was the first night I remember meeting Nicole.

Nicole, most recent member, since 2006: I remember strongly the first one I went to, it was at Michelle's house and the theme was New Orleans. I was so nervous because we had research our food item, and talk about how it related to New Orleans cuisine. My recipe was the drink, the Sazerac. I had so much to say about it because I was really thrilled with learning so much about a drink (I doubt many other drinks have such a history), but I was so nervous that I only managed to mutter just a few sentences about it. I was hoping they weren't going to kick me out of the club!

## What advice would you give someone who wanted to start a cooking club?

Dina: Be committed.

Michelle: Don't be afraid to challenge yourself in the kitchen, and to try foods you have never eaten before.

Cindy: Don't be mundane, and always try to think outside of the box. Push your fellow members to try new things and have fun!

Maria: Communicate your vision and be patient with each other because we all learn at various levels.

Lisa: To be adventurous and be willing to try new things.

Carolyn: Don't be afraid to experiment. That's what it is all about. You are doing this to learn, not because you are already an expert.

Nicole: Start with a few rules for the club. Otherwise it will fall apart from lack of cohesive plans.

## What is your greatest cooking club learning experience?

Dina: I'm comfortable entertaining in my home as a result of being in a cooking club.

Michelle: That every recipe you make doesn't have to be perfect. If you have a failure in the kitchen, it's actually not a failure at all, but a great learning experience that can be shared with the group. If a recipe doesn't turn out the way it should, talk amongst everyone in the group to find out what happened, and how not to do the same thing again. Many times, it wasn't the cooking club member's "fault" at all, but simply a poorly written recipe.

Cindy: That I can't do everything well. It is easy to think you can cook anything, but it is still a learning process. I ruined a panna cotta-like dessert at Lisa's because I didn't know how to work with gelatin. I was too cocky, thinking that I didn't need to read up on how to do it, and I ruined it by adding way too much gelatin. It is still a learning process and the more you try new things and get out of your comfort zone, the better you will be as a cook.

Maria: That we are all human with similar anxieties, who want to do well, and that it is okay to make mistakes; in fact, this is how we learn the best lessons and discover the best solutions. I have also discovered that I have a good sense of taste and smell, which helps me pair foods and wines well.

Lisa: That I'm willing to try new recipes and new ingredients that I would never have thought to try on my own.

Carolyn: I finally learned how to temper eggs with confidence!

Nicole: I have grown as a cook. I used to just do whatever I wanted with a recipe and thought that however it turned out would be good enough. Now I know that truly fabulous food is fabulous because of how it was prepared, in addition to the ingredients used.

## What is one tip you would give to help a cooking club run as smoothly as possible?

Dina: When it's my turn to host, I always start cooking club with an empty dishwasher. It makes cleaning so much easier.

Michelle: Having music playing before the first guest arrives sets the tone for the evening. I like to have the music pretty loud at the beginning to get everyone in a fun festive mood, and then to turn it way down while we are eating dinner.

Cindy: When it is your turn to host, really read the recipes, and think of the ingredients that go in it and plan before you make the menu. The thought process that goes into the menu and the individual dishes make the most successful gatherings. It's okay if the recipe was hard and it didn't turn out, you learn from that, but if the recipe doesn't taste good because it is just a bad recipe, then you know you can do better. And don't try to overachieve, because then your guests end up too full!

Maria: Test your main dish before the big event. It not only gives you confidence that it will be good but it allows you to work with it if it is a bad recipe. Most importantly, you can also plan the rest of the night's events based on both cooking and serving times for all other dishes being served. This also gives you the opportunity to see if you can make most of the dish ahead of time, allowing you to enjoy the night along with everybody else.

Lisa: Have a mix of people, like different ages, backgrounds, and professions, as well as different talents, from beginners to very experienced cooks.

Carolyn: Prepare early. Don't leave all the work for the day of the dinner. You will be too exhausted to enjoy it. Try and have all the work—housecleaning, shopping, and table set-up—done the day before. That leaves just the food and fun for the day of the dinner.

Nicole: Our club runs so smoothly because the members take it seriously. We have our schedule way ahead of time. We value keeping our commitment so we do whatever we need to so as not to let our fellow members down when it's our turn to host or attend the event. Showing up on time is always good, too!

# Index